Orwell's "Politics and the English Language" in the Age of Pseudocracy

Orwell's "Politics and the English Language" in the Age of Pseudocracy visits the essay as if for the first time, clearing away lore about the essay and responding to the prose itself. It shows how many of Orwell's rules and admonitions are far less useful than they are famed to be, but it also shows how some of them can be refurbished for our age, and how his major claim—that politics corrupts language, which then corrupts political discourse further, and so on indefinitely—can best be redeployed today. "Politics and the English Language" has encouraged generations of writers and readers and teachers and students to take great care, to be skeptical and clear-sighted. The essay itself requires a fresh, clear, skeptical analysis so that it can, with reapplication, reclaim its status as a touchstone in our era of the rule of falsehood: the age of "pseudocracy."

Hans Ostrom is Professor of African American Studies at the University of Puget Sound, USA. His previous publications include *A Langston Hughes Encyclopedia, Honoring Juanita: a Novel*, and *Metro: Journeys in Creative Writing*, written with Wendy Bishop and Katharine Haake. He has been a Fulbright Senior Lecturer at Uppsala University in Sweden.

William Haltom, Professor of Politics and Government at the University of Puget Sound, USA, teaches courses in politics and law. He is coauthor of *Distorting the Law* (Chicago 2004) and "The Laws of God, the Laws of Man: Power, Authority, and Influence in 'Cool Hand Luke,'" *Legal Studies Forum* (1998).

Routledge Studies in Rhetoric and Communication

For more information about this series, please visit: www.routledge.com

Orwell's "Politics and the English Language" in the Age of Pseudocracy

**Hans Ostrom and
William Haltom**

LONDON AND NEW YORK

First published 2018 by Routledge

2 Park Square, Milton Park, Abingdon, Oxfordshire OX14 4RN

52 Vanderbilt Avenue, New York, NY 10017

Routledge is an imprint of the Taylor & Francis Group, an informa business

First issued in paperback 2020

Library of Congress Cataloging-in-Publication Data
A catalog record for this book has been requested

ISBN: 978-1-138-49990-4 (hbk)
ISBN: 978-0-367-60717-3 (pbk)

Typeset in Times New Roman
by Apex CoVantage, LLC

Contents

Acknowledgments

We appreciate the conversations about Orwell we have had over the years with students and colleagues, especially at a colloquium with the Department of Politics and Government at the University of Puget Sound. Also at Puget Sound, discussions with colleagues in African American Studies have sharpened our thinking. We are grateful to the anonymous reviewer who assessed the manuscript for Routledge and us. We also thank the several colleagues with whom we talked about this project at the Law and Society Conference in Berlin and at meetings of the Western Political Science Association in Portland, Oregon, and Spokane, Washington. At the latter meeting, Professor Seán Patrick Eudaily (University of Montana–Western Montana) offered particularly helpful insights about a paper we presented that was related to the topic of this book. W. Lance Bennett surveyed a rough draft of Chapter 3 and offered guidance. The University of Puget Sound helped to fund our websites associated with this volume. Editors at Routledge/Taylor & Francis, including Felisa Salvago-Keyes and Christina Kowalski, have been most helpful, and we thank them.

Hans Ostrom
William Haltom
Tacoma, Washington, USA

1   Introduction

Be Careful What You Assign— Your Students Might Read It

George Orwell is well known to have legions of admirers who will leap to the keyboard to attack anyone who criticizes their hero. We academics are all supposed to admire him, and especially to regard his 1946 essay "Politics and the English Language" (henceforth P&EL) as a deathless masterpiece of political and literary insight, and to urge our students to read it. Two distinguished evolutionary biologists devoted recent blog posts to ladling renewed praises on P&EL. . . .

Well, apologies in advance to Orwell fans, but I have always found P&EL sickening. A smug, arrogant, dishonest tract full of posturing and pothering, and writing advice that ranges from idiosyncratic to irrational. Let me comment on just one of its sillinesses.[1]

As the overwrought characterization of Geoffrey Pullum above dramatizes, "Politics and the English Language"[2] may be at once the most celebrated and most castigated source regarding political communication in English-speaking letters.[3] We also suspect that fulsome praise and carping critique alike distract writers and readers from George Orwell's contributions to the betterment of communication. Celebrations and condemnations of rules and peeves neglect Orwell's major claim: Political decay and linguistic rot increasingly make each other worse. In the 21st century Orwell's admirers and his scoffers find themselves awash in immoral rhetoric and amoral rationalization created both for increasingly credulous audiences who expect fantasies and abhor facts and for increasingly distrustful audiences who take facts for falsehoods and falsehoods for facts.[4] Yet scoffers and admirers alike bring up clichés, metaphors, passive voice, jargon, or other small-bore matters that Orwell addressed[5] on his way to and from more momentous matters. Have we, the inheritors of Orwell's insights, squandered Orwell's bequest in "Politics and the English Language"? We regard this question to be rhetorical in more ways than one.

Attention to minor diversions in "Politics and the English Language" and neglect of major theses explain substantially but not completely both the essay's wide appeal and its near ubiquity in discussions of deceptive language, especially deceptive language in service of politicking, governing, and other aggrandizements. Orwell in his essay raised grave threats—politicos misuse language to make lies sound truthful and murders seem respectable—that the propaganda-laden 20th century and the image-suffused, fragmented 21st century exacerbated. Debasements of politics and language that he did and did not anticipate demand the attention of citizen and intellectual alike. By contrast, Orwell's rules for modern political writers around 1945, his excoriations of foggy phrases and mindless clichés, and his other gripes and gibes entertain his readers greatly but reduce decadent language or decadent politics little if at all.

Those who recall the essay may properly delight in its lampooning academic and bureaucratic prose, its accusing writers of "swindles and perversions," and its parodic dismantling of the pretentious and the precious, but such burlesque distracts and detracts from Orwell's most terrifying and compelling general portents, we maintain. His vaudeville distracts attention from corruptions of power, position, and prominence that matter far more than the parlance to which he drew attention. Moreover, the burlesques train his adherents to mock certain kinds of academic, bureaucratic, and politic expressions much the way that Comedy Central's Jon Stewart and Stephen Colbert did: with the very ironic infotainment[6] that suffuses public discourse. Such mockery may not always be politically impotent, but parody often inclines audiences to under-appreciate the plain appeal of imagery, dramaturgy, spin, symbolism, and propaganda. Consequently, some threats Orwell identified and other threats he did not foresee rule the political culture long after the laughter subsides. The parts of the essay too seldom recalled have been eclipsed by the wickedly entertaining parts such that "Politics and the English Language" has become barely political and almost entirely beside the point that he explicitly set for his enterprise.

We propose in this volume to rescue Orwell's obscured major point from Orwell's gaudy prose and the essay's fans. We also propose to transform his diagnoses and prescriptions into resources so that a classic 20th-century statement for writers may serve as a 21st-century guide for readers, viewers, listeners, and other "content-consumers" whom we take to be our immediate audience as well as for writers, producers, performers, and other "content-providers" whom he explicitly took for his immediate audience. In so doing, we introduce three ironies:[7]

Irony One—*The* Non Sequitur: Orwell's capacious claim at the beginning and end of his essay—that the decline of politicking and the decline of communicating reinforced one the other—barely followed from, led into, or even related to some of the essay's most memorable passages, yet that claim has proved reasonably prescient for reasons that Orwell could not have anticipated. Perhaps useless for political **writers** in 1945–46, the large-scale claim within which he elected to work might be very useful to political **readers** in the 21st century.

Irony Two—Gripes and Gibes: The gibes and gripes with which Orwell regaled his readers have proved so memorable that they are much more likely to be quoted or recalled than his momentous claim, so his piquant prose obscured his major point. Between his expansive pretext and extravagant postscript, he skewered doubletalk, euphemizing, and other practices in the infotaining but unenlightening manner of a pedant; his "catalogue of swindles and perversions," so often recalled or reproduced, distracted writers and readers alike from far more significant insights that underlay Orwell's intellectual infotainment.

Irony Three—Memorable Misdirection: Because Orwell highlighted six rules that were and are less useful or sensible than the six questions that he buried at the end of a long paragraph,[8] his writing pointed political writers to specific directives that could remedy neither general political and linguistic decline (his major, overall point) nor particular, recurring problems with political phrases (his intermediate-level point). Consequently the directives for which "Politics and the English Language" is often invoked have eclipsed his far more useful advice for students, readers, and writers.

These three ironies, separately and together, explain why and how critics and celebrants have largely squandered the most significant lessons of a classic document. We deem it bad enough that, owing to these ironies, those who read "Politics and the English Language" may long recall Orwell's drollery and parody but quickly forget his wisdom and especially his discernment. We deem it worse that those who revel in Orwell's particulars distract themselves from the larger concerns that he said he was on about. We deem it worst that lessons that might improve writing, reading, thinking, politicking, and governing in the 21st century fade from collective recollection even as familiar passages, tropes, and catalogues persist to abet pedantry.

Beyond these three ironies and taken as a whole, Orwell's "Politics and the English Language" makes evident and obvious sense less consistently than we might expect from a classic or than we might recall from reading it long ago. Orwell hastily assembled much of his case[9] and erred, but more problems and errors have followed from what readers, especially admirers, have done with the essay. He assembled a rickety framework that linked his peeves about writing to political decay in English or British politics. We think he hyped his piece.[10] Since 1946 the essay's shaky scaffolding has swayed but never toppled because the errant tropes, hackneyed phrases, phony grandiloquence, and other lousy writing against which he inveighed have persisted as objects of ridicule—the intellectual infotainment to which we referred—thanks in part to academics like us. "Swindles and perversions" (his hyperbolic terms) continue to present easy targets. However, such devices explain ever less about linguistic decadence, let alone political decay. Consequently, particulars have come to represent the essay while the larger concerns to which Orwell related the particulars have faded from many memories. Close readers of the essay dispute ever finer points and subtleties but may neglect not only more important issues in the essay but also the dominating ubiquity of propaganda, imagery, and truthiness.

To the degree any works of literature remain touchstones in 21st-century cultures, Orwell's does so. It not only retains its classic status, but it is still taught in colleges, and it is at least considered, even by detractors, as a foundation of works that concern bad writing. When we—an English professor and a political scientist—set out to address 21st-century political language, then, we saw the sense of starting with a foundational essay even in these anti-foundational times.

However, our aim is not simply to pay homage or indeed to pay any homage. Instead, we pay the essay the compliment of taking it seriously. We encounter anew its limitations and, more important, the effects those limitations may have had on generations of readers who barely recall the essay or the novel *1984* yet imagine they have a clear grasp of Orwell's wisdom and warnings. Additionally, as professors, we have observed generations of collegiate teachers in many disciplines who reenact the flaws of the essay when they allegedly teach students to write and to think critically. Such teachers often direct students away from critical thinking by overreacting to minor matters, as well as by enforcing personal preferences as if they were eternal verities of good writing and adept thinking.

We wrote this book, then, for all the readers and all the teachers who have come upon or may come upon "Politics and the English Language." Orwell purported to write for political writers, British writers, or writers in general. These content-creators, he thought, could recreate and thereby revive the English language, which had decayed owing to bad habits of writing and thinking. If writers could break their bad habits of writing and thinking, the language and thought of the polity might be improved, he hoped. This might make politics, governance, and society work better. We aspire to revive the best and most important lessons and exhortations from the essay to the betterment of those who consume communications. We aim our book at readers who watch television and films, tweet and text, and experience media created after 1945. We write for those who listen to radio and who still read newspapers and books. We think that "Politics and the English Language" still has much to offer more than half a century after its appearance. We hope this book will help those who read (and those who assign) that classic to get as much of Orwell's wise counsel as we can highlight.

To see the steps by which we hope to reach our audience, let us anticipate the rest of our book.

Rereading "Politics and the English Language": Chapter 2

Rereading "Politics and the English Language" closely and critically after the manner of its fierce critics, we question our own high regard for the essay, which seems to cohere fitfully at best. Orwell repeatedly wrote and argued in ways that seem to us insincere or incompetent. He violated his own strictures too often for his rules to be credible.[11] We marvel that an essay we have read so many times and assigned our students over the years can be as flawed as careful analysis reveals it to be. It seems the celebrity of the essay blinded us.

Our goal in Chapter 2 is not to besmirch the classic or to write ill of the dead. Rather, we intend to show how many praises heaped on "Politics and the English Language" are unmerited but also how merits of the essay often go unremarked if not unnoticed. We scrub the essay of its vices so we can recognize its virtues. For one chapter, we join those who carp at a classic so that in later chapters we may refurbish the essay's legacy.

We identify vices and virtues via analyses of the essay. We schematize the structure of "Politics and the English Language" and anticipate that our graphing will startle many teachers who have assigned the essay because of fond recollections rather than recent re-familiarization.[12] Once our readers see that in the first two and last four paragraphs of his essay Orwell unmistakably states that his overall point is that linguistic and political decline mutually reinforce, they may ask how intermediate paragraphs bear on his self-proclaimed mission. This establishes for our readers Irony One, which, as suggested above, we occasionally label *The* **Non Sequitur**.[13] We then read those 13 intermediate paragraphs carefully to reveal that, entertaining and evocative as they are, they relate to the overall point that Orwell set himself in the essay far less than they reiterate the notes from which he was working. Between his resounding opening[14] and restrained closing,[15] he sandwiched his gripes and gibes about usage in a "catalogue of swindles and perversions" and an inventory of euphemisms. This close reading exposes Irony Two, the intermediate-scale incongruity we sometimes label "**Gibes and Gripes**." It also shows more connections between his gibes and gripes and his list of rules than between those complaints about usage and any other points Orwell advanced. These connections help demonstrate how his six questions have much more to do with the essay as a whole and with good writing and reading than do his six ballyhooed rules: Behold what we sometimes call the "**Memorable Misdirection**" of Irony Three.

Chapter 2 confirms Orwell's own judgment that the remainder of his essay "follows" at best a shaky logic. In about 5,000 words Orwell conducted his readers from the systemic, sociological causes of mutually reinforcing political and linguistic decline to six rules for better proofreading, so the essay's trajectory plunges into trivial fussing. In what we hope to be an assessment more charitable and productive, however, we argue that he began his essay with a doozy of a diagnosis—the decay of the English language and of the British polity explained each other; we further claim that he provided specific symptoms of decadence in political writing and politicking. The intermediate part of "Politics and the English Language," the filling between the slices of his overall thesis, presents examples of empty phrasings, mental vices, and thinking enthralled by conformity and convenience. Having identified a syndrome of poor writing and worse politicking, Orwell declared in his last four or five paragraphs that political writers should remedy specific symptoms of horrid prose on the way to repairing the general political decay from which his essay started.[16] While we dispute his invocation of cause-and-effect regarding politics, governance, and expression and demur from his specific "evidence," we think his classic can be rescued. That presumptuous rescue is what we attempt in Chapters Three through Five, which take up in turn the three ironies we have posited.

Saving the Whole From Memorable Particulars: Chapter 3 and Irony One

Having disassembled the overall argument of "Politics and the English Language" in Chapter 2, in Chapter 3 we reassemble the whole in a new context to show that Orwell provided writers and especially readers a more useful perspective than, we think, he could have known, especially if we extend "readers" to listeners, viewers, and other consumers of content in the 21st century. Whatever he thought about correcting habits of political writers to brake or reverse decay, his attitude in exposing con games and linguistic legerdemain—an attitude we call "discernment" throughout this book and especially in Chapter 5—furnishes in our view his largest-scale and most promising contribution to politicking and to speaking, writing, and reading the U.S. variant of the English language. That attitude, we concede, has not reversed or braked decay; political and linguistic decadence may even have increased. After all, Donald Trump is at this writing President of the United States and has rested Orwell's case.

However, we argue that Orwell's attitude provides a formidable remedy for political and linguistic decline in our own time, provided we can extract Orwell's overall attitude from his vivid, aphoristic, and thus all the more distracting particulars. Chapter 3 thus addresses and perhaps redresses Irony One: that the large-scale framing of his essay, perhaps useless for political writers in 1945–46 and maybe counterproductive, might yet prove useful to political readers in the 21st century.

To reclaim Orwell's overall thesis, to make the argument of his essay more cogent, and to adapt his insights to 21st-century language politics, we show in "You Can't Handle the Truthiness: How 'Politics and the English Language' Suits Our Times Better than Orwell's Decaying Britain" how evolving "pseudocracy"[17] leads to truthiness. By "pseudocracy" we mean that shams, pretenses, and mendacity dominate political language and public discourse related to politics and create rule by falsehood. Some pseudocratic domination matches Orwell's critique of language abuses, as when catchphrases and shibboleths[18]—for instance, "Got Hope?" or "death panels"—dominate discourse not despite but owing to their deficiencies or deceitfulness. Other pseudocracy involves more than slipping down slopes of convenience or conventionality. Technologies of advertising and marketing, of broadcasting and narrowcasting, of suasion, and of electioneering have revolutionized languages and polities alike to the point that few or no words need be uttered or written. Combinations of politicking, governing, marketing, electioneering, and reporting closely simulate democratic traditions even as they bemuse citizens, obliterate subtlety, spread lies, perpetuate fantasies, avoid data, disrupt policy-making, law-making, campaigning, and opinion-leadership, and distort definition of problems and formulation of solutions. Orwell lamented that political writers were gumming prefabricated phrases together; nowadays consultants fabricate phrases selected with the help of focus groups and present those phrases alongside images that encourage viewers to believe that they have seen proof and truth.

Not only have public relations, political image-making, and consumer-culture since 1946 greatly diluted the culture of public intellectuals and literary citizens about whom and to whom Orwell wrote in his essay, but mass education and mass media have also driven societies, especially the United States, to widespread apathy and inattention, infotainment and sensationalism, and reaction and distraction. On the Internet and immersed in social media, current-events enthusiasts now parrot talking points and succumb to frames that persist long after the short-run advantages that shaped them fade. Modern education and modern media have made informed, thinking, involved citizens ever more susceptible to propaganda because of their felt need, self-induced and fanned by political operatives, to stay "informed," "up-to-date," and "relevant." That need in turn makes them ingest more and more products of the pseudocracy even as mass media and opinion leaders misinform citizens far beyond the ability of fewer and fewer objective, thoughtful, competent writers to remedy.

Enter truthiness. Writers and readers in the 21st century are both passive spectators who selectively (mis)take infotainment for truth and active collaborators in suiting selected truths to their preferences and preconceptions and even their whims. Writers, readers, and viewers come to prefer ideas or to treat as facts what we wish were true or want to be true, rather than ideas or facts held to be true by persons in position to verify truth.[19] This truthiness breaks down unified and unifying societal truths that writers and readers may take for granted into truths both partial and partisan.[20] Multiple, mutually inconsistent renderings of reality create competing, conflicting truths to which factions can cling and can conform their politics and their language.

We suspect Orwell never thought that pseudocratic propaganda, spin, and deceptions might sharply reduce both the possibility and the need of flat-out lying. So many deliberate untruths are held by many Americans to fall short of lying that almost every leader or celebrity will have defenders who contest whether the accused or the assaulted "truly lied," "misspoke," "stretched the truth," "spun," or was "taken out of context." Worse, within the pseudocracy, dishonesty everywhere is candidly acknowledged almost nowhere and, when admitted, usually overlooked. Worst, truthiness drives the polity and the vernacular so much that lies not only sound truthful but are truthy, and murders are not merely respectable but necessary, to redeploy two flourishes from the essay.[21] Add ever-present media and appetites for instant, simplistic responses that crowd out public intellectuals and experts in favor of battling pundits and crosstalk, and solid information evanesces even as pure wind—another phrase from the essay—blows consistently.

Appreciation of pseudocracy and truthiness makes irrelevant many of Orwell's most memorable presumptions and observations—the particulars and aphorisms for which his essay remains renowned—yet makes Orwell's overarching premise all the more pertinent to the present context. That is Irony One. For Orwell to argue that "politics itself is a mass of lies" was glib in the 20th century but is almost irrelevant in the 21st-century US society in which talking points, pseudo-events,[22] and the like have made lying usually unnecessary and even artless; nonetheless, his resistance to mendacity—one of his attitudes we consistently praise—pertains even more to today's pseudocratic, truthy pronouncements. Perhaps it made some sense for him to claim that "[i]f you simplify your English, you are freed from the worst follies of orthodoxy . . ." before sound bites, but Frank Luntz and other professional propagandists have oversimplified English so that it serves orthodoxies right and righter.[23] Writers, readers, and viewers can deflect some of the worst follies of orthodoxy individually and perhaps even in groups by abhorring empty abstractions and by exposing ambiguous expressions—other Orwellian attitudes we repeatedly praise—rather than by abhorring passive voice or lamenting clichés.

Rescuing Orwell's Essay From Memorable But Misleading Infotainment: Chapter 4 and Irony Two

Once we have rescued Orwell's overall design in Chapter 3 from difficulties we raised in Chapter 2 by reading Orwell as critically as he read and advised us to read other political writers, we turn in Chapter 4 to rescuing "Politics and the English Language" from the very phrases and passages most often invoked by admirers and detractors. First, we dispense with those often-recalled elements that are and always were, we demonstrate with rue and embarrassment at our having assigned the essay, misleading. Then we turn to resounding aphorisms and passages that constituted solid advice to political writers and especially readers of all things political. Indeed, given the pseudocracy we posited in Chapter 3, some of Orwell's observations become more pertinent in the 21st century than when he wrote the essay amid the 20th century. Even lessons and pronouncements that were wrongheaded, we show, may have become useful.[24]

Chapter 4 begins from the intermediate irony that many parts of "Politics and the English Language" are revered when they should be rejected. We deal in detail with three of the most renowned and misunderstood missteps. First we show that Orwell adduced five examples that must trouble anyone who inquires into them, so it may be for the best that admirers of the essay give no evidence of having inquired into them. Having shown his "prosecution" of his five specimens to be at best an overreach, we show that his "catalogue of swindles and perversions," while far worthier of attention than his five "specimens," features much humbug alongside ample punctiliousness amid myriad minutiae. This, according to us, makes Orwell not only an "Overreaching Prosecutor" but also an "Overbearing Pedant." Third, we show why his academic or bureaucratic parody of the King James translation amuses if a reader glosses over it but troubles if a reader reflects on it.[25] Enter "Orwell the Overlooking Parodist."

Having counseled readers to think less of some of the very parts of the essay that have made it famous for so long, we then advise readers and other content-consumers to think more about lessons that lie beneath the showy but defective devices. That is, we show aspects of the essay that deserve to be revered. Orwell's five not-very-representative examples point at errors that every author should avoid but do not suggest tactics that conscientious authors should disdain and competent readers detect. We salvage from his "catalogue of swindles and perversions" tactics most deployed amid the pseudocracy to foment truthiness; these of course include stratagems developed since the essay's publication (1946) and Orwell's death (1950). We then show how the poetry of the King James Bible and the precision and accuracy of bureaucratic parlance might together meet the demands of political communication and citizenship in the 21st century more than either could separately.

The specimens, the catalogue, and the parody illustrate the intermediate irony we noted: The very gibes and gripes with which Orwell regaled his readers concealed significant insights behind infotaining folderol. As we did in Chapter 3, in Chapter 4 we rescue his attitude from his use of political language and show how the habits of mind and the vibrant skepticism that drove him can yet drive readers and Internet writers to seek truth from, as well as speak truth to, power.

Recasting Questions and Rules Into Understandings: Chapter 5 and Irony Three

In Chapter 5 we return to Orwell's ballyhooed rules and buried questions so that we may explore our third, most specific irony: Orwell's questions promise far more clarity and thoughtfulness than his rules, yet his questions are usually overlooked in favor of his rules. While we agree that Orwell's questions offer readers and writers too little guidance, we strive in Chapter 5 to snatch from his lists some lessons worthy of him and of a classic.

We argue, for instance, that Orwell's first and fifth rules are poorer guidance for writers and readers than three of his questions.[26] More important, we advise readers, as they heighten their awareness and sophistication, to analyze intended audiences rather than merely words and phrases loosed at audiences. We further suggest that readers and writers alike analyze themselves to discern, for example, the extent to which, like almost everyone, they may be easy targets for some talking points, catch phrases, slogans, shibboleths, argot, and clichés. And finally we suggest that readers analyze one more crucial element of rhetoric: purpose. What is the object of communication and communicator?

Hence, our aim in Chapter 5 is to guide our readers in understanding why communicators communicate as they do so that readers, viewers, and listeners might do something concrete about down-spiraling politics and language. Orwell stated that his rules and questions might better enable writers to begin to reverse the decay of politicking and communicating. We offer evidence and argument from his own essay why such reversal is unlikely to come from political communicators: Any communicators who practice the sincere, candid, responsible, and ethical writing that he recommended will easily be defeated by communicators who practice insincere, cunning, irresponsible, and unethical writing. We therefore argue that realistic remedies will more likely be found in equipping audiences to expose mystifications, their own as well as those of others. Chapter 5 argues that better reading is the means by which the better writing Orwell counted on might be more than the panacea that he offered.

In Conclusion: We End Our Beginning

Untwisting three ironies we perceived and one classic Orwell created, we aim in the chapters ahead to refurbish "Politics and the English Language" to suit 21st-century readers and writers. To contemporary instructors we propose how to glean from the essay its enduring lessons so that contemporary pupils might profit from it more than our pupils have over the decades. To contemporary readers we propose how to attend to the perils Orwell identified without becoming ensnared in needless, arcane disputes about trivialities semantic or pedantic. To contemporary writers we propose how to disregard ill-phrased and unhelpful rules in favor of better-phrased and helpful questions matched to stages of composition. We hope what we supply will increase demand to make Orwell matter even if we have to remake his essay to derive the attitudes, aptitudes, and habits that instructors, readers, and writers should learn from him.

As we identify issues large and small in Chapter 2, reconsider Orwell's expressed larger-scale strategy in Chapter 3, rehearse some smaller-scale tactical issues in Chapter 4, and worry fine-grained mechanical issues in Chapter 5, we interject suggestions about how our readers and we might remedy the political and linguistic decay Orwell saw and the decadence he did not foresee. Our suggestions twist his contentions into a more realistic, more personal bent by deriving from his essay the attitudes, aptitudes, and habits that individuals and perhaps communities might acquire and sustain.

Individually, in small groups, and in coalitions, political communicators can ameliorate some dire circumstances that Orwell presumed and other malignancies that even he could not foresee; they cannot remedy systemic, structural, long-range decay. Readers and writers may be able to rescue themselves and their correspondents from pseudocracy, imagery, and mendacity; they cannot save their larger culture from the mendacity, pseudo-events, propaganda, and infotainment that suffuse mass media, electioneering, and governments.

Hence this book focuses more on writers, viewers, readers, and listeners than on politics and other imperious institutions. However much sense it made for Orwell to address fellow pundits and public intellectuals in 1945, his essay has become a classic via its assignment to earnest, young, or at least ingenuous communicators. We concentrate throughout on how readers may decode and demystify political communication amid a raging, enraged pseudocracy. In Chapter 4, for example, we reconsider metaphors and, more generally, tropes to derive the attitudes and aptitudes that make readers and writers discerning. Orwell famously endorsed colorful figurative images, but in the 21st century, vivid imagery and figurative language are problems at least as much as solutions. As pseudocracy substitutes sound bites for thought and imagery for argument, vibrancy and stridency of expression menace the clarity, concreteness, and candor for which Orwell pleaded. What he advocates writers to select, we advise writers and readers alike to suspect. Lurid, arresting images or phrases usually tantalize. They titillate and entertain but rarely deliver true insight or actionable intelligence. In place of lurid writing, we counsel the relentless realism Orwell manifested when he demanded concreteness. If a word on a bumper sticker, a phrase in a slogan, or a trope in the message of the day offers clear references that might be checked against consensual observations and theories, the reader, viewer, and listener may justifiably attend to it. If the talking points or policy salvos have far more to do with focus groups, partisan spin, depraved appeals, or ideological shibboleth than with any commonly shared reality to which the communicator explicitly, clearly commits, then readers, viewers, and listeners must steel themselves to reject it and, more important, overcome it.

In the 21st century, it follows, readers, viewers, and listeners must avoid sound bites and other morsels that are propounded to confound and must seek out communicators who are as honorably clear as Orwell rightly advocated that writers be. Only in this way might con artists be outcompeted by competent, candid communicators. In Chapter 5 we proclaim Orwell's lonely truth-telling and relentless candor to be his "master habit" (a culmination of his attitudes and his aptitudes) that we two would have our students and Orwell's readers acquire and hone.

We should not expect that Orwell, who denounced political discourse rife with lies and rationalizations, would have advised writers to avoid deceit and distortion, for he might have regarded such as axiomatic. Thus, we exhort instructors and others who would enhance their personal discourse (as opposed to impervious systemic discourse) to caution readers to expect the misinformation and disinformation that teem amid the pseudocracy and to teach students and readers to resist tides of mendacity, blather, and authoritarian populism. Resorting to Internet fact-checkers, we note at multiple points, is now a basic precaution for sensible citizens. We review resources already accessible for 21st-century audiences and recommend that writers, professional as well as avocational, thoroughly acquaint themselves with mass media that check misinformation, disinformation, and especially the kinds of faulty information writers are most likely to overlook, forgive, or support.

Further, we demand that content-providers and content-consumers adopt expectations that are among the greatest legacies of academia: attention to sources and to sources' veracity. This is our refurbishment of Orwell's persistent preference for the concrete. In the 21st century deliberate deceit costs prominent writers and politicos little. If critical citizens would reward truth and penalize deception, they must learn to keep score, and so we preach the old-time religion of evidence and authority. We propose to surmount Orwell's memorable misdirection by focusing more on the truths that Orwell articulated and the attitudes that he prosecuted than on his opinions about vivid or moribund metaphors, his opaque if not instantly moribund metaphor "verbal false limbs," and other fake scents and nonsense.

Orwell's tips do bloggers, posters, people who never raise their eyes from smart phones, and other 21st-century writers little good and 21st-century readers almost no good. Moreover, the very immediacy, ephemerality, and attention-grabbing that excite detractors of newer media promise infotainment that may match the messaging and framing which presently dominate and degrade our polity and language. We stress an attitude of discernment as an answer. The essay's specimens, catalogue, and parody evince an attitude that equips readers and writers to resist political and linguistic decline. We want those who read the classic to learn his discernment and to discard, largely if not entirely, his devices unworthy of his discernment.

Many of the most decadent forces in our political and linguistic communities will in effect quarantine themselves if discerning and truth-seeking citizens commandeer modern, more participatory mass media for their own conversations and conversions. We cannot eliminate the lies and euphemisms that Orwell rightly denounced, but through blogging, tweeting, and conversing after the manner of George Orwell we can expose lies and euphemisms in our own politicking and governing. This is especially the case in our local politics and language. Societies that abound in truthiness tend to segregate audiences by their preferences for what they want to be true over what most informed persons acknowledge. It follows that the more that putative knowledge is restricted to a party, faction, or clique, the less entitled to factuality the putative knowledge may become.

We exhort our readers to guard zealously and jealously the ideas and inferences that they deem knowledge and, when in doubt, to push lies, euphemisms, dramaturgy, imagery, sound bites, talking points, and other banter and badinage back into zones of misinformation and disinformation. We believe that "Politics and the English Language"—properly updated and sympathetically understood—may abet and assist that resistance.

Notes

1. Geoffrey Pullum, "Elimination of the Fittest," *Lingua Franca* (blog), April 8, 2013, accessed February 14, 2015, http://chronicle.com/blogs/linguafranca/2013/04/08/orwell-and-the-not-unblack-dog/. Useful as Professor Pullum's thunderbolt is to convey passions that "Politics and the English Language" yet stirs among academic and literary natterers, we think he protests too luridly.
2. Orwell wrote the essay in late 1945. It appeared in *Horizon*, April 1946, accessed December 2, 2017, www.orwell.ru/library/essays/politics/english/e_polit; and in George Orwell, "Politics and the English Language," *The New Republic*, June 17, 1946, 872–874 and June 24, 1946, 903–904.
3. The prominence of the essay more than half a century after its publication attests to its timelessness, albeit that in our third chapter we argue the essay timelier in the 21st century than in the 20th. Readers who are skeptical of the essay's endurance may want to look at two recent collections of Orwell's essays. Jeremy Paxman wrote that the 1946 essay "remains the best starting point for anyone hoping to achieve the deceptively hard task of clear communication." Jeremy Paxman, "Introduction," in *Shooting an Elephant and Other Essays* (New York: Penguin Books, 2003; introduction copyright 2009), ix; George Packer, "Foreword," in *All Art is Propaganda: Critical Essays* (New York: Mariner Books, 2009), xii included the following sentence: "Aside from 'Politics and the English Language' and perhaps 'Shooting an Elephant,' none of his essays are widely read, and some of the best remain almost unknown." May the coauthors also recommend the very first sentence of Hugh Rank, "Mr. Orwell, Mr. Schlesinger, and the Language" in *College Composition and Communication* 28, no. 2 (1977): 159–165?
4. To see how an audience may at once regard facts as falsehoods and falsehoods as facts, see Farhad Manjoo, *True Enough: Learning to Live in a Post-Fact Society* (New York: John Wiley & Sons, Inc., 2008), 224–225.
5. Please note that, in this book, we do not follow the convention of referring to an author who died in 1950 or an essay first published in 1946 by means of the present tense. We are aware that for many readers Orwell's choices in his essay survive and Orwell in some way(s) continues to set out words he set down in 1945. We acknowledge that we are fussy to fret about the tangles to which use of the perpetual present might lead.
6. We have more to say about "infotainment" later in this book; for now we use "infotainment" to denote a compounding of information or news with entertainment. We note as well that a common connotation of "infotainment" is that news or other information is shaped more by the objects and formats of entertainment media than the medium or story is shaped by the facts or data.
7. We use "irony" to denote our formulations that embrace contraries, and we acknowledge that "irony" has multiple meanings in 21st-century usage. Please substitute "twists" if you like.
8. We shall see throughout this book that Orwell routinely violated his own rules but not his own questions.
9. According to the table of contents in Peter Davison, ed., *The Complete Works of George Orwell* (Volume Seventeen, "I Belong to the Left 1945") (London: Secker & Warburg, 1998), vii–xiv, Orwell in 1945 wrote at least eight essays other than "Politics and the English Language," at least 30 articles, at least 51 reviews, at least seven "As I Please" columns, and dozens of letters. Excluding

the letters, we count at least 96 writings in 1945. We cite this record to indicate that Orwell wrote quickly and often in 1945. We defer to editor Peter Davison's judgments about what counts as an essay, a review, a column, or an article.

We find it amusing that Volume Eighteen of *The Complete Works of George Orwell* (London: Secker & Warburg, 1998) carries the title "Smothered Under Journalism 1946." The year 1945 looked plenty smothering to us!

Please keep in mind that, before Orwell published "Politics and the English Language," he published in "As I Please," his column in the *Tribune*, some of his challenges to current writing. For earlier versions of some of Orwell's peeves, please see George Orwell, "As I Please," *The Tribune*, March 17, 1944, accessed July 20, 2012, www.netcharles.com/orwell/essays/asiplease1944-03.htm#Mar17; and George Orwell, "As I Please," *The Tribune*, February 9, 1945, accessed July 20, 2012, www.telelib.com/authors/O/OrwellGeorge/essay/tribune/AsIPlease19450209.html. It follows that Orwell may have thought about "Politics and the English Language" repeatedly and for some time.

10. Indeed, Orwell inflated the stakes of his essay in the manner of a future President: "People may not always think big themselves, but they can still get very excited by those who do. That's why a little hyperbole never hurts. People want to believe that something is the biggest and the greatest and the most spectacular. I call it truthful hyperbole." Donald J. Trump and Tony Schwartz, *Trump: The Art of the Deal* (New York: Ballantine Books, 2015), 58. There, we think, the parallels between Orwell and Trump end and the sharp contrasts begin.

11. We realize that Orwell admitted he violated his own rules. We insist, however, that the more often Orwell diverged from his own commands for competent, clear prose, the more he reduced his own credibility or authority in prescribing rules for other writers.

12. We entitle this introductory chapter "Be Careful What You Assign—Your Students Might Read It." The great danger that we dare not write in a chapter heading is that students read what we instructors assign without ourselves rereading!

13. "Non sequitur" is Latin for "it does not follow." Once common in collegiate vernacular, the phrase is nowadays less common. It stands for inferences that are less than logically compelling.

14. See paragraphs one and two in the telescoping graphic introduced in Chapter 2 and archived at politicsandtheenglishlanguage.info.

15. Paragraphs 16 through 19, "Telescoping Diagram" at politicsandtheenglishlanguage.info.

16. Hugh Rank notes as well Orwell's reliance on metaphors of disease and cure. See Rank, "Mr. Orwell, Mr. Schlesinger, and the Language," 160.

17. "You can't handle the truthiness" combines a memorable line from Jack Nicholson's character in the film *A Few Good Men* and the coinage, "truthiness," by Stephen Colbert in his parodic television show, *The Colbert Report*.

18. By "shibboleth" we mean a characteristic of communication that marks or identifies some group of persons as "us" or "them." The term derives neither from Ancient Greek nor from Ancient Latin but from Hebrew. See in the King James Version of the Bible the Book of Judges Chapter 12, verses 4–6.

19. The American Dialect Society defined truthiness as "the quality of preferring concepts or facts one wishes to be true, rather than concepts or facts known to be true." Please see accessed June 21, 2014, www.americandialect.org/2006/01. We slightly rephrase that definition of the "2005 Word of the Year" in our main text above.

20. To see that we are not engaging in hyperbole, please see Manjoo, *True Enough*; and Jennifer L. Hochschild and Katherine Levine Einstein, *Do Facts Matter? Information and Misinformation in American Politics* (Norman, OK: University of Oklahoma Press, 2015).
21. "Political language—and with variations this is true of all political parties, from Conservatives to Anarchists—is designed to make lies sound truthful and murder respectable, and to give an appearance of solidity to pure wind."
22. Chapter 3 will define "pseudo-events;" for present purposes we mean by "pseudo-events" opportunities for visual, audio, or verbal communication that are created to be disseminated and designed more for audiences not physically present than for immediate audiences.
23. Frank I. Luntz, *Words That Work: It's Not What You Say, It's What People Hear* (New York: Hatchette Books, 2007); George Lakoff and Elizabeth Wehling, *The Little Blue Book: The Essential Guide to Thinking and Talking Democratic* (New York: Free Press, 2012). In the 1990s, Dr. Luntz worked for Rudy Giuliani, Pat Buchanan, Ross Perot, and Newt Gingrich. Dr. Luntz invented the term "death tax" to describe a tax on inheritances and "climate change" to replace "global warming." See Molly Ball, "The Agony of Frank Luntz," *The Atlantic*, January 6, 2014, accessed December 9, 2017, www.theatlantic.com/politics/archive/2014/01/the-agony-of-frank-luntz/282766/.
24. We find it ironic that the most momentous claim in Orwell's essay should be doomed by the modern culture of mass communications that the essay resembles. That is, Orwell's essay is to a degree infotainment, entertainment masquerading as information.
25. Orwell is entitled, of course, to his opinion that "[t]his is a parody, but not a very gross one." The authors find the parody broad, facile, and misleading but droll. We concede readily that some of Orwell's readers might admire it more than we do.
26. "Never use a metaphor, simile, or other figure of speech which you are used to seeing in print" is Orwell's Rule #1 and "Never use a foreign phrase, a scientific word, or a jargon word if you can think of an everyday English equivalent" is Orwell's Rule #5. Orwell's questions include "2. What words will express (what the writer is trying to say)?" and "3. What image or idiom will make it clearer?" and "4. Is this image fresh enough to have an effect?"

Bibliography

American Dialect Society, The. "Word of the Year." Accessed June 21, 2014. www.americandialect.org/2006/01.

Ball, Molly. "The Agony of Frank Luntz." *The Atlantic*, January 6, 2014. Accessed December 9, 2017. www.theatlantic.com/politics/archive/2014/01/the-agony-of-frank-luntz/282766/.

Davison, Peter, ed. *The Complete Works of George Orwell* Vol. 17, *I Belong to the Left 1945*. London: Secker & Warburg, 1998.

Davison, Peter, ed. *The Complete Works of George Orwell* Vol. 18, *Smothered in Journalism 1946*. London: Secker & Warburg, 1998.

Hochschild, Jennifer L., and Katherine Levine Einstein. *Do Facts Matter? Information and Misinformation in American Politics*. Norman, OK: University of Oklahoma Press, 2015.

Lakoff, George, and Elizabeth Wehling. *The Little Blue Book: The Essential Guide to Thinking and Talking Democratic*. New York: Free Press, 2012.

Luntz, Frank. *Words That Work: It's Not What You Say, It's What People Hear*. New York: Hatchette Books, 2008.

Manjoo, Farhad. *True Enough: Learning to Live in a Post-Fact Society*. New York: John Wiley & Sons, Inc., 2008.

Orwell, George. "As I Please." *The Tribune*, March 17, 1944. Accessed July 20, 2012. www.netcharles.com/orwell/essays/asiplease1944-03.htm#Mar17.

Orwell, George. "As I Please." *The Tribune*, February 9, 1945. Accessed July 20, 2012. www.telelib.com/authors/O/OrwellGeorge/essay/tribune/AsIPlease19450209.html.

Orwell, George. "Politics and the English Language." *Horizon*, April 1946. Accessed December 2, 2017. www.orwell.ru/library/essays/politics/english/e_polit.

Orwell, George. "Politics and the English Language." *The New Republic*, June 17, 1946, 872–874, continued June 24, 1946, 903–904.

Packer, George. "Foreword." In *All Art is Propaganda: Critical Essays*. New York: Mariner Books, 2009.

Paxman, Jeremy. "Introduction." In *Shooting an Elephant and Other Essays*. New York: Penguin Books, 2003.

Pullum, Geoffrey. "Elimination of the Fittest." *Lingua Franca* (blog), April 8, 2013. http://chronicle.com/blogs/linguafranca/2013/04/08/orwell-and-the-not-unblack-dog/.

Rank, Hugh. "Mr. Orwell, Mr. Schlesinger, and the Language." *College Composition and Communication* 28, no. 2 (1977): 159–165.

Trump, Donald J., and Tony Schwartz. *Trump: The Art of the Deal*. New York: Ballantine Books, 2015.

2 Rereading "Politics and the English Language"

We hope Chapter 1 articulated our overall claims in this book and anticipated how Chapter 2 will serve those claims with more specific ones. Overall, we believe that "Politics and the English Language" is and deserves to
be a classic. We second Orwell's explicit call to all writers to be more inten-
tional about their motives and their words. We extend that call and invite
readers to demand more precision, clarity, and honesty from what they read.
For decades the title of the essay, if not the work itself, has served as a
virtual meeting place where people converse about imperfect prose arising
from unworthy motives and faulty habits. In our book as in this chapter we
enter that meeting place to converse precisely, clearly, and honestly about
"Politics and the English Language."[1]

To be honest, clear, and precise, we contend that the essay is a muddle—
something its status and that of its author often obscure. In this chapter we
show that most of the famed parts of the essay do not suit the whole as
tightly as they might and that many parts entertain more than enlighten.
The essay's most momentous major claim is served poorly when it is served
at all by such features as Orwell's five "specimens," by his catalogue of
four "swindles and perversions," by his six "rules," and by his unnumbered
gibes and gripes.

In this chapter, we will "read" Orwell's essay from afar, and then reread it
close up. Our "far reading" will establish that, taken in as a whole, "Politics
and the English Language" barely coheres. Our closer readings will reveal
that, taken part by part, "Politics and the English Language" is seriously
flawed even if we call it "an informal essay" and note that it was dashed off
amid frenzied productivity by Orwell. We will relate many of the flaws in
parts of the essay to the three ironies shaping our book. We will note as well
flaws that do not bear directly on our three ironies or the classic essay as a
whole but will leave for later chapters thorough examination of those flaws.

Our telescoping diagram at politicsandtheenglishlanguage.info/telescope.
html should enable you to refresh your recollection of "Politics and the

English Language," if you wish to do so, as well as to enhance your appreciation of its features.

Taken as a Whole, "Politics and the English Language" Barely Coheres

Before we engage in a close reading of the essay, we present a reconstruction of it in the following table.

Table 2.1 Far Reading "Politics and the English Language"

Section	Word count	Paragraph(s)	In this section George Orwell primarily . . .
I	341	1–2	Diagnoses the problem of mutually reinforcing decadence in politics and language and prescribes shedding bad habits of writing as a "necessary" first step toward political regeneration.
II	686	3–4	Adduces five "fairly representative examples" that illustrate the mental vices that make for poor English and claims that staleness and imprecision are vices common to the examples.
III	1,300	5–8	Defines and illustrates "swindles and perversions" rampant in contemporary writing, especially political writing.
IV	449	9–10	Produces then analyzes a parody of a passage from the King James Bible to insist that modern prose lacks concreteness, simplicity, and vividness.
V	674	11	Summarizes shortcomings of modern prose's reliance on hackneyed phrases rather than words carefully selected for clear and precise meanings, and then rehearses such lack of clarity and precision in the five "specimens."
VI	987	12–15	Generalizes that conformity to orthodoxy deadens prose through euphemisms, incorporation of convenient presumptions, and vagueness, with the result that correct thinking corrupts writing, which in turn corrupts thinking.
VII	1,018	16–19	Reminds readers of Orwell's diagnoses and prescriptions from paragraphs one and two, notes two examples of clichés jeered away, denies that prescriptions are pedantic, introduces six rules that will remedy most of the vices and all five of the "specimens," and reiterates that clear, concrete, vivid, precise, and accurate writing will remedy some of the mutually reinforcing decay of language and politics.

"Politics and the English Language" consists of approximately 5,400 words, seven sections, and, by our count, 19 paragraphs. To see how we dissect the essay, please refer to Table 2.1, which reveals that parts of the essay support its major contention reasonably well for a comment quickly written and published but less impressively than we might expect of a classic to which scholars frequently allude or to which they send their students.

In his first two paragraphs (Section I in Table 2.1) and his last four paragraphs (Section VII in Table 2.1), Orwell explicitly diagnosed poor writing and sloppy thinking and prescribed small first steps by which to remedy the mutually reinforcing bad habits devastating language and polity. Statements of the diagnosis and prescription to a great degree conform at the essay's beginning and ending. Orwell's essay thus appears unified. Our closer reading later in this chapter will reveal flaws in that apparent unity.

If the beginning and the ending correspond, the fit of the paragraphs between the beginning and the ending seems far from tight. Orwell claimed that five "fairly representative specimens" of prose as habitually produced each evinced stale images and imprecise descriptions (Section II), which might lead more generally to fusty, fuzzy writing, speaking, and thinking. Orwell's catalogue of swindles and perversions (Section III) followed his five examples and exemplified linguistic degeneration that Orwell claimed to endanger England and English. Orwell's parody of a passage from the King James Bible (Section IV) burlesqued contemporary writing, but Orwell's demonstrating that Elizabethan poetry cannot survive more prosaic expression suited neither directly nor well Orwell's general points about stale, imprecise prose and decadent politics or governance. When Orwell speculated about behavior or psychology that might have led to bad habits among political writers (Section V) and used his speculations to explain the lack of clarity and precision in the five "specimens" of Section II, he tried to reunify his wide-ranging, entertaining criticisms. In Section VI, he moved from behavior and psychology to a more societal explanation. He mused how the imitation of unreflective, automatic expression might promote conformity, docility, and convenience, so that poor prose hid or euphemized unconscionable decisions and behaviors. In Section VII, Orwell concluded his essay by reiterating his diagnosis and formulating his prescriptions as rules for writing.

Exacting readers will have noticed that Orwell diagnosed a two-way relationship between politics and language at the start of his essay but prescribed a one-way fix by the end of his essay. In general, "Politics and the English Language" advances a systemic diagnosis but offers only piecemeal remedies.

The essay's logic may seem to "beg the question," but we do not assign such a fallacy to Orwell's essay. Although Orwell presumed that the lazy, facile repetition of socially or politically prescribed phrases and beliefs impaired language and governance alike, that presumption, as we read the essay, diagnosed symptoms of what was ailing politics and language. After presenting the symptoms, he in effect described a syndrome, a chronic, systemic relationship between poor writing and poor politicking. Once he had linked symptoms to a syndrome, he proposed palliatives.

Our analysis of the essay's structure and logic anticipates the three ironies mentioned in Chapter 1. Orwell began his essay from his diagnosis of the syndrome and ended it with his prescription for treating the syndrome. His thick diagnosis and thin prescription make the essay more than a mere collection of complaints about writers' relying on ready-made phrases. Yet, to the extent that his memorable, amusing plaints greatly outshone his start and his finish, our three interrelated ironies become hard to gainsay. Even in the synopsis of our far reading, Orwell sandwiched attention-arresting "specimens," alarming "swindles and perversions," appalling euphemisms, and a parody between two paragraphs of diagnosis and four paragraphs of prescription. This sandwich induces generations of readers to attend more to Orwell's filling—his gripes and his rules—than to the thick slice that preceded and the thin slice that succeeded the gripes and the rules. Ironically, then, Orwell made his essay less sustaining intellectually even as (indeed because) he made its delicious filling easier to recall and to extol. He overshadowed his systemic diagnosis and prescription (our large-scale first irony) with attention-grabbing harpoons and lampoons (our intermediate-scale second irony) and, even more so, with six rules that bear barely if at all on the serious, mutually reinforcing political and linguistic problems from which he began his essay (our small-scale third irony).

Our Closer Readings Disclose That, Part By Part, "Politics and the English Language" Falls Apart

Barely tenable read from afar, Orwell's argument becomes flatly untenable if read closely and carefully, which we must never have done before assigning the essay to our students. What may be worse, Orwell consistently faulted the English used in contemporary writing in such an entertaining, vivid manner that the enticing parts tumble out of the whole if readers are not distracted from the whole by the arresting parts. As a result, many of his funny gibes and amusing gripes detract from a reader's close, careful understanding of his larger argument. Indeed, the more that his curmudgeonly snark delights readers as it does us, the more likely it is to distract readers and writers and us from his wholesale diagnosis and retail remedies. Unpersuasive if read carefully and holistically, Orwell's classic is unlikely to be read either carefully or holistically owing to the quality or qualities of its components.

As we justify our sour assessment above, we close in for a part-by-part analysis. We refer to our telescoping graphic (available at politicsandtheenglishlanguage.info) so that our readers may check our work. The rightmost column of that graphic reproduces the essay verbatim. The leftmost column reiterates the sectioning that we covered in Table 2.1 above. In the column in between we synopsize the essay paragraph-by-paragraph. These distillations constitute and guide our closer reading of "Politics and the English Language."

Our Close Reading of Section I—Orwell's Diagnosis Remains Trenchant

In our "far reading" of the essay as a whole, we applauded Orwell's first two paragraphs. Alas, we must now fault Orwell's second paragraph for the disheveled manner with which it ends. As Orwell elaborated his diagnosis and pronounced political and linguistic decay reversible, he tossed off this clunky transition: "I will come back to this presently, and I hope that by that time the meaning of what I have said here will have become clearer. Meanwhile, here are five specimens of the English language as it is now habitually written." These two sentences evince hasty writing, and who among us has not written something similar in an early draft? That Orwell hoped his meaning would have become clearer later in the essay reflected a passivity beyond the passive voice that his fourth rule proscribed; it showed some diffidence about the intermediate parts of his essay. As we shall see below, that diffidence was well-founded.

Nonetheless, the first two paragraphs of the essay clearly linked English politics to English and proposed a remedy to the decay of each. Section I stated Orwell's mission. Admirers and detractors of the essay alike should acknowledge that Orwell clearly set out a diagnosis and asserted that the disease was treatable. These issues seem to us worthy of serious reflection. That, indeed, is why we have formulated Large-Scale Irony One, the *"Non Sequitur."*

Our Close Reading of Section Two—Orwell's "Specimens"[2] Begin Orwell's Humbuggery

In his third paragraph (by our count; see the rightmost column of the telescoping graphic), Orwell adduced "five specimens of the English language as it is now habitually written." If we scan "specimens" neither closely nor critically—which is what we two must have done for years—they each and all illustrate mental vices he imputed to writers later in the essay, which makes the essay flow deceptively smoothly. In our closer reading, by contrast, the "specimens" do not establish how English was habitually written and do not represent political writing, but those failings we consider carefully in Chapter 4. In that chapter we find the "specimens" to constitute striking, memorable symptoms of assumed mental vices that do not constitute convincing examples of political writing in Orwell's time or our own. For now we sketch our "findings" about how flawed Orwell's articulation of his stated thesis and his five specimens was.

1. Professor Laski's sentence, far from English as it was habitually written in 1946, was not typical even of the rest of Laski's chapter, let alone of Laski's publishing or British letters in general.[3] If Orwell adduced the Laski "specimen" to represent habits of prose and of mind common among political writers, he was committing the "sheer humbug"[4] of which he accused others; if he quoted Laski's "specimen" to set up observations about mental vices and to entertain, he made his composition flow at considerable cost to coherence and cogency.

2. Orwell likewise entertained but misled his readers if his second "specimen" was supposed to represent political writing or English as habitually written. He ripped a sentence from an eccentric zoologist's formulation of an artificial language to represent common vices or habits of mind? This showed mutually reinforcing decline of politicking and communicating how?

3. Orwell's third "specimen" in like manner illustrated mental vices but could scarcely be thought to typify writing in general or political writing in particular. This sentence, too, exemplified impenetrable academic argot and, thus, more of Orwell's own humbuggery but lacked any pertinence to his systemic diagnosis.

4. The Communist pamphlet ("specimen" four) might have served Orwell better later in the essay to illustrate deleterious effects of pretentious diction and orthodoxy on and in Marxist writing but scarcely bore on mental vices in general or some characteristic turn in British letters, as he must have known.

5. The letter to the *Tribune* ("specimen" five) may have presented amusingly flawed writing that Orwell attributed to mental, behavioral, or social vices but strikes us as more an attempt at humor than a point at all germane to the diagnosis that he explicitly set out in Section I.

Orwell's "five specimens of the English language as it is now habitually written" could never have established mental vices, habits of mind, or social malaise commensurate with the scale of his diagnosis in paragraphs one and two of his essay. The gross mismatch of scale between the general diagnosis and five selected symptoms impaired Orwell's argument from its start, we are sorry to observe. (We wonder how we missed this over the years.) His "specimens" are cunning and instrumental diversions but far from representative or persuasive. They constitute infotainment in which entertainment values far outstrip the value of the information. Orwell's infotainment is droll and sophisticated relative to 21st-century infotainment, we admit. Over the decades the entertainment value in ridiculing three professors, one or more political operatives, and a letter-writer doubtless encouraged instructors to assign the essay and invited those outside academia to use the essay to bash academics. But the more that the ridiculed illustrations conduct readers into mental vices that Orwell wants to assert and the less that the ridiculed illustrations represent political writing, the more humbuggery he tosses off and as he begins to offer evidence.

Our Close Reading of Section III—Orwell's Catalogue of Orwell's Hobbyhorses

Even if Orwell's "specimens" had persuasively evinced a "mixture of vagueness and sheer incompetence [that] is the most marked characteristic of modern English prose, and especially of any kind of political writing"—they do not, but we do not demonstrate that until Chapter 4—the "catalogue of swindles and perversions" that followed them seems to us coauthors to illustrate writers' laziness (and Orwell's haste!) more than writers' haziness or incompetence. Orwell adduced examples in which writers created prose far from lively or precise and gummed his five "specimens" to his "catalogue"[5] by noting how writers settle for hackneyed phrases instead of choosing the correct word or words to express their meanings precisely. How such habits result in systemic politicking and systemic language he did not state, so this third part of the essay amuses but exacerbates the misfit between his particulars and his general point.

Although we greatly esteem Orwell's general insight that poor writers tend to opt for preformulated phrases while better writers tend to craft words to express their thoughts, items in Orwell's catalogue of swindles and perversions satisfy us less. In Chapter 4 we demonstrate that his gibes and gripes entertained more than enlightened; that each of his peeves insufficiently accounted for political decline; that he seldom stated which devices were to be deemed swindles, which perversions, and which simply labor-saving devices for writers. Our examination of the catalogue's particulars, in sum, inclines us to insist that the very delights of his ridicule divert. The catalogue delightfully diverts students and instructors with droll or raucous scorn yet often diverts his readers from the diagnosis with which he started and ended his essay.

Our Over-Reading of Section IV—Orwell's Parody Amounts to Horseplay for Horselaughs

Orwell's rewrite of a passage from the King James Bible is quite humorous and thus memorable. If we are correct, the parody of Ecclesiastes is too memorable. We find it hard to regard Orwell's wry waggery as germane to system-wide politics, governance, or habits of writing any more than the "specimens" in Section II or the "catalogue" in Section Three. Beyond that assessment of increasing incoherence in the essay and exacerbated irony, especially for our intermediate-level, second irony, we belabor the parody in detail when we get to Chapter 4.

Our Close Reading of Section V—Orwell's Summary

After his rollicking presentation of impertinence and impertinents in paragraphs three through ten (also known in Table 2.1 above as Sections II through IV), Orwell summarized his case for symptoms that make up the syndrome of decadent politicking and writing to which he alluded occasionally. In pursuit of convenient phrasings, preset rhythms, and facile affectation, he claimed, writers deny readers and themselves clarity, precision, and sometimes even meaning through prefabricated phrases, mixed metaphors, or other thoughtless prose. Indolence and expedience might explain the five specimens and the swindles and perversions. Careless writers might express likes or dislikes with little concern for or even interest in how they express them. By contrast, careful writers would trouble themselves to figure out their meaning and how best to express it clearly, vividly, and succinctly without avoidable ugliness. Orwell concluded that careless habits of mind and expression led to thoughtless politics while more conscientious use of language would lead to more thoughtful politics. He then appended to an already long paragraph six questions that a conscientious writer would ask himself or herself.

His summation is more persuasive than the infotainment that preceded it, but is that summation as memorable or as cited as the entertaining "evidence" that he purports to summarize? Our answer, we hope it is evident, is "Not so much." Does Orwell's earnest, methodical presentation in paragraph eleven atone for or redeem the masterful flimflam of paragraphs three through ten? We do not think so. Why have we and other instructors assigned students to read an essay in which a famous author entertainingly misdirected readers for roughly eight paragraphs and almost 2,500 words and then crammed his (borderline) respectable arguments into a single paragraph of barely more than one quarter as many words? More, what do readers who encounter "Politics and the English Language" for the first time get from Orwell's six questions pinned as a tail onto that eleventh paragraph?

Our Close Reading of Section VI—Orwell Introduces His Parts to His Whole; Together Again for the First Time

Having asserted that modern writing reflects indolence and indifference of writers, Orwell in his next four paragraphs associates bad writing with bad politicking, thereby returning himself and his readers to what he had said he was setting out to argue. The second paragraph of the essay forecast this return to his diagnosis that declining habits of writing and declining modes of politicking worsen each other. He now began to link poor writing to poor politicking, albeit luridly. He did not settle for the claim that orthodox, conformist writing tended to make thoughtful humans less thoughtful. Rather, he conjured in paragraph 12 an insidious opposite to infotainment: When "some tired hack" recites orthodox, conformist speeches in which there are only familiar phrases and nary a "fresh, vivid, homemade turn of speech," the speaker transforms thoughtful humans into thoughtless automatons. In the next paragraph Orwell arrayed current atrocities screened from uncritical audiences by the sorts of ready-made and often government-issued phrases that since have been called "Orwellian." He denounced such "euphemism, question-begging and sheer cloudy vagueness" that obscured the brutality and motivations of leaders and states. Beyond strategic and tactical communication Orwell saw a menacing, general impulse: "The great enemy of clear language is insincerity." He had shown already that repetition and imitation of hackneyed expressions clogged writing; now he insisted that clichés and catchphrases numbed the brains of those who read them and those who wrote them.

By the end of this sixth section of the essay, Orwell related the indolent habits of writers about which he had written in earlier sections and the strategic phrasings of political hacks that he had been excoriating in the present section in a manner that aggregated his diagnosis, his infotaining examples and speculations, his serious arguments, and the psychological, sociological, and political effects of slovenly, sloppy writing and thinking. This aggregation of themes established his diagnosis, which justified a turn to his prescribed remedies.

In sum, our close reading of Section VI shows that Orwell resumed the exercise in macro-diagnosis and micro-prescription that we noted in Part One. That correspondence of mission in Section I and execution in Section VI, of course, throws into even starker relief the absence of such correspondence in Sections II through V, which by our count consist of 3,109 words (2,487 words if the number of words in the "specimens" is excluded) and nine paragraphs.

Our Close Reading of Section VII—Orwell's Prescriptions Are Palliatives

Having completed his diagnosis in the four paragraphs of the sixth section, Orwell moved in the four paragraphs that we have assigned to the seventh and final section to stating and justifying his prescription for the interplay of poor writing and poor politics. As noted, his prescriptions have narrower gauge than his systemic diagnosis in Section I. Let us now investigate the degree to which he hyped in Section I and downplayed in Section VII.

Orwell's Modest Fixes

At the very start of paragraph sixteen, Orwell explicitly heralded his transition to prescriptions for acting on his diagnosis. He identified some bad habits of writing that small groups had or might have extinguished through ridicule, but admitted that those particularities were minor matters. Then he moved to sketch a larger-scale defense of the English language by fending off misreadings of his essay.

Orwell's Defensive Ripostes

Orwell's anticipating and refuting objections to his prescriptions added some jerkiness to his essay, for the reader who endured at least seven peeves in paragraph sixteen that Orwell promptly confessed were minor matters now must face another delay as he lavishes five sentences on those who might mischaracterize the remedies that he had yet to prescribe. In our reading of the essay, therefore, let us hurry past five sentences of Orwell's defenses so that we may get to a) the general prescription that he tucked into the midst of paragraph seventeen; b) the model of and for writing that he provides immediately after his general prescription; and c) the rules that he prescribed to guide writers when they are uncertain. Our close, critical reading will show each sort of prescription to be both inadequate to remedy the systemic problem that Orwell has defined and debilitated by his own imprecise, pretentious writing.

Orwell's Model of Composition

Orwell's general prescription appears in the sixth and seventh sentences of paragraph seventeen: "What is above all needed is to let the meaning choose the word, and not the other way around. In prose, the worst thing one can do with words is surrender to them." Throughout, the essay Orwell has protested that lazy, thoughtless writers too often settled for prefabricated phrases rather than proceeding word by word to express their thoughts clearly and precisely, so this prescription suits a general tendency that he has excoriated. Our close reading has shown (and in Chapters Four and Five will show in more detail) that he repeatedly failed to choose his words to insure clarity or precision, but that does not gainsay Orwell's insistence that he should have. What does gainsay his general prescription is that he is suggesting that lazy, thoughtless writers stop being lazy and thoughtless. The suggestion that writers who produce substandard copy by "gumming together long strips of words which have already been set in order by someone else, and making the results presentable by sheer humbug" discipline themselves to proceed thoughtfully and systematically word by word is at least optimistic.

What also gainsays Orwell's general prescription is Orwell's model of and for writing. Orwell presumed that methodical, mindful writers form their thoughts wordlessly and then select words that suit their thoughts. Most academic writers and other professional writes, teachers of writing, and students in high school and college would probably model the process of composition as a far more dialectical negotiation between inspirations and formulations and be less sure of a difference between "thought" and "language." (And the way writing has been taught in high school and higher education in the United States, Canada, and Great Britain, especially after the 1970s, has emphasized a dialectical and recursive process.) From this view of writing, the very difficulty that Orwell identified—words selecting meanings—is an inextricable part of formulating thought and perhaps even of the processes of thinking dialectically and reflectively. His advice, then, may not be merely impracticable but impossible for writers and for readers. There is little use here in taking a detour into philosophical questions about thought and language, but we ought to note that to think a thought probably requires a mental engagement with language even before speaking or writing occurs.

Orwell's Gaudy, God-Awful Rules

Whatever one's view of Orwell's general prescription and his recommendations for methodical composing, Orwell's six rules for writers seriously, serially compromised the aims for which Orwell prescribed them. Reading each rule closely shows us that he failed to phrase even one of his rules adequately! In Chapter 5 we cover at length how he failed to phrase each rule to the standards he imposed on other writers; for now we assert that all the rules are defective.

We also show in Chapter 5 that each of Orwell's six rules is deficient judged against one or more of the questions that Orwell appended to paragraph eleven back in Section V. If his often-recalled rules fail of the standards implicit in his seldom-acknowledged questions, that is for the coauthors' immediate concern a matter of less importance than that Orwell's six rules (even if complemented with his six questions) each and all seem minuscule before systemic political decline that Orwell had diagnosed. If readers take the malady that he diagnosed to be systemic and important and real, his rules and other particular prescriptions would seem to promise relief, at most, even if he or anyone phrased them more carefully. Indeed, such prescriptions might make patients more comfortable amid an epidemic, which might be worse than accepting our inability to stanch or reverse the debilitating condition he had identified.

To summarize our analysis of Section VII: Orwell's prescriptions turned out to be palliatives at best.

Summing Up Our Close Reading

If Orwell's individuated, particular prescriptions for writers seem a palliative for the systemic, general malady that Orwell diagnosed at the start of his essay, then our close reading has revealed more of a mismatch between problem and solution than our far reading disclosed. Nor is this mismatch between diagnosis and prescription(s) the only difficulty that close reading turned up. If we fill in the outline of the essay's general logic with particulars noted through close reading, "Politics and the English Language" seems even more uneven than we claimed at the beginning of this chapter.

The Whole and the Parts of "Politics and the English Language" Have Led to Three Ironies

Our analyses of the essay have uncovered its roughly logical main line and far rougher relationships between or among its parts and that main line. When we beheld the essay from afar, we found that the main line consists in a diagnosis of the systemic decline of politics and English, a marshaling of evidence or arguments about the decay in writing and its relation to decay in politics and governance, and general or specific prescriptions to halt or reverse the decline in politics and English. When we examined the marshaling of evidence or arguments and the prescriptions general and specific more carefully, we found the cogency of some sections or paragraphs suspect and some sections, paragraphs, or sentences to be insightful and others to be incitements. What to make of the larger and small parts and of the whole?

Concerning the essay as a whole, our closer reading reinforced a feature that we saw even via our far reading: Orwell recommended minute remedies for what he billed as widespread declines. His general remedy—writers should choose their words to suit the writers' intended meaning rather than settle for familiar, thoughtless phrases that skew writing toward orthodoxy—might be quixotic if it were not so piecemeal. The most capacious cure(all) he offered had little chance of slowing or stopping the decline of English because political writers or writers in general are unlikely to overcome the mass of users of English. And what of the mass of politics? "[P]olitics itself is a mass of lies, evasions, folly, hatred, and schizophrenia," so writers should choose their words painstakingly?

Despite its narrowing at the end, the essay as a whole diagnoses widespread, mutually reinforcing links between politics and language.[6] We regard this "syndrome" as the essay's most important general insight. We also see the connectedness of language and politics as the most important lesson our students might derive from reading the essay. We concede that the essay has more specific rewards for students and other readers, but we urge our readers to acknowledge that Orwell's opening diagnosis is momentous even if his closing recommendations are mincing.

What is more, Orwell expended 40%–47% of the words in his essay (depending on whether we count the words that make up the five "specimens" or annotations or italicized examples that appear amid passages devoted to diagnosis or prescription) on his "specimens," his "catalogue," and his parody. For that reason alone we might expect many readers of the essay to take from it this uproarious quotation, that "swindle" or "perversion," or that droll parody. However, we suspect that his stinging rebukes made the habits of prose and mind memorable as well. Whatever the explanation for the persistence of what we have shown to be very flawed features of his essay, we regret that our students and others have recalled those features more often and more vividly than his overarching point.

That is the origin of Irony One, *The* Non Sequitur. The main line of logic in the essay elicits less attention than parts of the essay that we have shown to be at best problematic. We acknowledge the persistence in the minds of students and scholars alike of virtuous aphorisms or assertions. Those sentences or passages reduce the first irony a bit, we concede. Still, we insist that Harold Laski or Lancelot Hogben or other academics brandishing verbal false limbs menaced politics and English far less than euphemisms for murder or excuses for conformity.

This broad, primary irony relates to a smaller, secondary irony: Orwell's peevish, pedantic infotainment can so captivate our students and other readers that they may miss superior insights and obvious shortcomings. Many of our students recall the "catalogue of swindles and perversions" because Orwell listed four categories that are easy to take notes on and to reproduce in a paper or an examination. Almost no student, to our knowledge, has noticed that he failed to identify which were the perversions, which the swindles, and which mere repetition or emulation or pretentiousness. An inarticulate dullard can say, "Huh?" at the end of Professor Laski's cavalcade of negatives or the letter-writer's screed, but the spotlight that Orwell directed toward such flawed writing may push into relative twilight such obscenities as "pacification" as a term for murdering the helpless and destroying any means of subsistence for survivors or "population-relocation" for dispossessing the weak of their lands and possessions or similar defenses of the indefensible that are among the signal contributions of this classic essay (and far more important components of what people ought to mean by "Orwellian" than his dystopian novels). This is our Intermediate-Scale Irony Two: For some readers, infotaining pet-peeves upstage insights that are far more important for the readers' political and linguistic educations.

Our third irony is less important but, alas, more famous; it provides memorable misdirections. Orwell set off his list of rules for writers from the end of his third-to-last paragraph. This, we presume, accounts for the frequency with which the six rules have been reproduced word for word.[7] The setting off of the six rules may also account for the lesser currency of his six questions for scrupulous writers to ask themselves. We argue in Chapter 5 that inexperienced writers likely will take his rules too seriously or ignore them altogether and that some modulated, sensible weighing of those rules is the most challenging and therefore least likely result for inexperienced writers. By contrast, experienced writers likely will overlook Orwell's rules because they will know that the rules make no sense **as rules**. Inexperienced and experienced writers alike, we shall argue, will find in his questions more and better guidance than in his rules. That is an irony we see.

For each of our three ironies, we expect that the expertise and savvy of readers will affect the import of the irony. Experienced writers and readers—Orwell's apparent targets, please remember—likely will breeze past systemic alarums that Orwell sounds at essay's start (thereby diminishing in Irony One); likely will disregard his fussy, fusty cavils (thereby dismissing many gibes and gripes and thinning Irony Two); and likely will heed what he meant by his rules and questions more than what he wrote (thereby overcoming or at least ameliorating Irony Three).

Conclusion: A Classic Flawed Yet Iconic

"Politics and the English Language" is a classic and deserves to be. Since 1946 it has called on writers to be more critical of their motives and their words and, by extension, has invited readers to ask more precision from what they read. For over six decades, the title of the essay, if not the essay itself, has warned us that imperfect prose arises from imperfect motives and slovenly habits. Its observations and formulations about politics and language retain relevance. However, latter-day readers must discern the enduring virtues of this classic essay amid prose that is slovenly, imperfect, imprecise, and at places ill-motivated—something its status often obscures. Parts of the essay do not suit the whole as tightly as Orwell might demand of other writers. Some passages entertain more than enlighten. Passages, paragraphs, sentences, phrases, and words are one or more drafts from the clarity to which he exhorted others. Perhaps worse, he drifted considerably from one of his main points—that politics and language seem to have entered into a pact of mutually assured destruction—into pedantry and even self-parody.

Let us assure those who, like ourselves, cherish the essay that what is muddled about the essay need not affect its status. Its flaws may make the work endearing, and we esteem many works both iconic and flawed. Indeed, we reassure ourselves that Orwell, were he alive and able to slog through our prose, might applaud at least some of our criticism of his essay both because in it he conceded that he exhibited the same failings for which he faulted other political writers and because after listing five rules for writers, he added a sixth rule that gave writers leave to break his first five. The spirit revealed by these two rhetorical moves suggests to us that Orwell, unlike some of the essay's fans, didn't regard his essay impervious to criticism.

Notes

1. We have set out our favorite passages. Please see Hans Ostrom, "Main Points, Revisited, of Orwell's Famous Essay," *Politics and Language* (blog), June 23, 2012, https://politicsandlanguage.wordpress.com/2012/06/23/main-points-revisited-of-orwells-famous-essay/; and William Haltom, "The Core of Orwell's 'Politics and the English Language'," *Politics and Language* (blog), June 20, 2012, https://politicsandlanguage.wordpress.com/2012/06/20/the-core-of-orwells-politics-and-the-english-language-2-2/.

2. We consistently enclose "specimen" between quotation marks to remind ourselves and our readers that Orwell opted for a term that might connote an almost scientific approach, when Orwell's examples serve at best as metonymy or synecdoche. Excoriating "pretentious diction" in his seventh paragraph, Orwell disapproved words that were "used to dress up a simple statement and give an air of scientific impartiality to biased judgments." The coauthors find "specimen" to be such a word.

3. Orwell purported to count five negatives in Professor Laski's 53-word sentence. Gary N. Curtis finds at least six. See Gary N. Curtis, "Untie the Knots," March 2, 2010, accessed June 15, 2012, www.fallacyfiles.org/archive032010.html#03022010. We give Orwell the benefit of the doubt: to count "not unlike" as a single negation is not unreasonable.

4. In our main text we appropriate a sentence from paragraph 11: "It consists in gumming together long strips of words which have already been set in order by someone else, and making the results presentable by sheer humbug."

5. We do not know what to make of Orwell's calling his list of complaints a "catalogue." We surround his term with quotation marks to remind our readers that, as with "specimens," Orwell himself engages in pretentious diction belied by the four complaints he adduced.

6. Orwell explicitly presumed that political decline led to linguistic decline, which in turn made politics worse, and so on. We have no idea how Orwell would know

that politics or language began to slide first. We presume that he needed to start his "negative feedback loop" with one or the other. Charging politicos with original sin is convenient in an essay ostensibly aimed at writers.

7. We wonder if Mr. Orwell would have permitted us to use "verbatim" in place of "word for word." We are accustomed to seeing "verbatim" in print, and "verbatim" comes from Latin *verbatim*. Verbatim is shorter than "word for word."

Bibliography

Curtis, Gary N. "Untie the Knots." March 2, 2010. Accessed June 15, 2012. www.fallacyfiles.org/archive032010.html#03022010.

Haltom, William. "The Core of Orwell's 'Politics and the English Language'." *Politics and Language* (blog), June 20, 2012. https://politicsandlanguage.wordpress.com/2012/06/20/the-core-of-orwells-politics-and-the-english-language-2-2/.

Ostrom, Hans. "Main Points, Revisited, of Orwell's Famous Essay." *Politics and Language* (blog), June 23, 2012. https://politicsandlanguage.wordpress.com/2012/06/23/main-points-revisited-of-orwells-famous-essay/.

3 You Can't Handle the Truthiness

How "Politics and the English Language" Suits Our Pseudocracy Better Than Orwell's Decaying Britain

This chapter concerns Orwell's large-scale diagnosis in "Politics and the English Language."[1] Although this diagnosis usually elicits less attention than Orwell's list of rules or his "vivid" phrases, it is among Orwell's greatest contributions in his essay. If it was less apt for political **writers** in 1945–46 than for political **readers** in the 21st century, and if the opening and closing paragraphs of the essay offer the diagnosis more as pretense than as presumption, "Politics and the English Language" still suits our times better than Orwell's. In Chapter 1 we labeled this twist "Irony One."

But in this chapter we first show that the diagnosis from which the essay begins is a not-very-apt pretext for Orwell's "catalogue of swindles and perversions" and his other jibes and jabs. It even less aptly represents how political élites and their operatives shaped writers and writing. According to our large-scale reading and rendering, Orwell flashed attitude at writers and writing and then used his own aptitudes for debunking to serve his own attitudes. If Orwell had detailed more fully methods by which élites and their operatives orchestrated "messaging," the clichés and euphemisms of which he complained would have appeared trivial relative to marketing and propagandizing in practice by 1945–46 when Orwell wrote the essay. We marshal insights from theorist Jacques Ellul concerning propaganda amid the 20th century and from celebrity and politician Donald Trump concerning factional truthiness to understand the advanced image-making and deceit that we label pseudocracy, the rule of falsehoods. We conclude by noting that **the "change in attitude"[2] about which Orwell speaks at the end of his essay is a suitable remedy for his diagnosis of mendacity only if applied by and to both writers and readers to create an aptitude for debunking the rule of imagery and falsehoods**.

We fear readers who do not attend to Irony One will misuse Orwell's classic. Dead within five years of dashing off his essay, Orwell could neither revise nor reconsider. When he paraded pretext and then flaunted semantics, Orwell did what essayists often do: He tantalized readers with a provocative opening, and then switched to the actual message. We think we owe it to readers to translate or at least to contextualize the essay. Beyond Irony One or because of Irony One, we must take responsibility for what we and other readers do or should do with this classic essay. We must salvage from the essay what we deem best. That is what we are on about in Chapter 3.

In Table 3.1 we preview three practitioners who will assist us in elaborating this analysis: George Orwell, Jacques Ellul, and Donald J. Trump. We maintain that each of the three adopted an attitude toward élites' "top-down" communications. We understand élites to include elected officials, CEOs of large corporations, extremely rich political donors, party leaders and insiders, military leaders, those who control and front large media concerns, and celebrities.[3] We ascribe to Orwell a "semantic attitude" in which—reading down the left column of Table 3.1—linguistic swindles and perversions dominate politicking and writing because élites induce writers to disengage the critical sensibilities of readers even as writers' habits numb writers' sensibilities. We then remind our readers that Orwell's Semantic Attitude misrepresented how modern élites deployed public relations and democratic imagery. We adduce Jacques Ellul's analyses of propaganda amid the 20th century to show that élites simulated bottom-up politics by orchestrating expressions of beliefs and practices—reading down the central column of Table 3.1.[4] Ellul showed how such élites corrupted communication to serve top-down designs, matched journalistic and commercial imperatives of truly mass media, and inculcated in masses a need for the messages that élites and media disseminated. The last is perhaps Ellul's most important contribution to seeing communication more as a system and less as questionable semantics.

If Orwell's semantic quibbles thus did not correspond to how states and systems deployed communication in the 1940s, Orwell's linguistic emphases feature far more relevance for the 21st century. In the 21st century, Donald J. Trump has shown (see the right column of Table 3.1) how political forces might use cunning formulations to shape reality to match the interests and preferences of élites and cliques, to meet the needs of spinners in mass media, and to satisfy the desires of credulous and even rabid consumers who identify with the cliques. Trump's "Truthy Aptitude," then, has reflected Orwell's diagnosis of systemic decline through semantic dodges (the Orwell attitude), and it has reflected Ellul's dissection of systematic domination through top-down design of beliefs and practices (the Ellul attitude). Trump partakes of the habit if not the system of customizing facts and truths to the ends, wishes, and fantasies of factions: Trump's attitude and aptitude. To the extent that politics and language have in the 21st century devolved to "truthiness," Orwell's diagnosis of political, linguistic culture attains far more pertinence than when he wrote it.

Table 3.1 Preview of "Attitudes" and "Aptitudes" in Communication Systems

	Orwell's Semantic Attitude	Ellul's Systemic Attitude	Trump's Truthy Aptitude
Dominant Content	LINGUISTIC SWINDLES AND PERVERSIONS **displace** concrete, clear, and candid expressions to the detriment of both politics and language as well as truth, understanding, clarity, and sense.	ORCHESTRATED ORTHODOXY AND ORTHOPRAXY **surround** audiences with multimedia messages and images that reinforce one another, arouse and calm by turns, and conform masses' actions and beliefs to regimes' designs and legitimation.	CUSTOMIZED ALTERNATIVE REALITIES **conform** perceptions and interpretations to polarized, prefabricated viewpoints that cohere in mass media, groupthink, and echo chambers to fragment factuality.
Purveyors	ÉLITES, PARTIES AND POLITICOS **dispense** clichés, euphemisms, abstractions, lies, and blather that reduce critical intelligence and defend indefensible top-down (mis)rule.	ÉLITES AND PROPAGANDISTS **choreograph** verifiable or at least not disprovable information, misinformation, and disinformation to legitimize top-down rule as if it issued from bottom-up consent.	CLIQUES AND FACTIONS **disseminate** truths adapted from and to their group realities through disparate media to "authenticate" realities or to make realities arguably populist or both.
Conveyors	POLITICAL WRITERS **supplant** vivid, candid descriptions and observations with prefabricated phrases to suit the convenience, expedience, and thoughtlessness of writers as well as the designs of (mis)leaders.	MASS MEDIA **transform** communication through images, immediacy, and abstractions that disengage critical faculties, incite actions, and create needs, expectations, and satisfactions.	SPINNERS AND CASUISTS **coevolve** truths and groups through tested, tailored slogans and shows that harden cleavages, and affirm truth-holders while they defame truth-rejecters.
Consumers	READERS [we presume] **accept** prefabricated phrases as substitutes for concrete, harsh facts and **acquiesce** in élites' (mis)rule owing to misleading or masking usages that numb readers' brains.	CURRENT-EVENTS MAVENS **need** and **expect** current, credible stories and imagery to make them appear critical and intelligent consumers of information and shapers if not makers of important decisions in the polity.	TRUE BELIEVERS **need** and **expect** "new" reports to reinforce set identities, cleavages, and views of in-group and to refute images, issues, and views of opponents as counterfactual.

Section One—Orwell's Obvious Pretext, His Less Obvious Semantic Attitude, and Our Own Responsibilities in Assigning "Politics and the English Language"

"The great enemy of clear language is insincerity."[5]

Orwell's Obvious Pretext—We begin from a flaw in the essay that Orwell might have denounced in any other writer. As he implicitly acknowledged, he began "Politics and the English Language" from a pretext that did not describe aptly politicking and writing in the 1940s. He formulated a large-scale diagnosis that served in 1945–46 and thereafter more as a creditable motive for advancing his particulars and peculiarities than as a representation of how political élites and their operatives amid the 20th century shaped writers and writing. In this section, we review that large-scale diagnosis— we label it "Orwell's Semantic Attitude"—and contrast it with piecemeal palliatives that fill out the rest of the essay and may have been the greater impetus for him to write the essay.

In the first two and last two paragraphs of his essay, Orwell implicitly confessed that the mutually reinforcing decay of English politicking and the English language at most framed grumbles and guidelines that made up the bulk of his essay. His systemic opening claim and his specific gripes, jibes, questions, and rules barely pertained one to the other, but he concocted a "Semantic Attitude" to make his particulars appear pertinent to his large-scale diagnosis. This pretext was and is pretense. Whatever its simulation or dissimulation of coherence or cogency amid the essay, that Semantic Attitude bore little resemblance to interrelations of politics and language in Orwell's time. As previous chapters disclosed, he walked back in his closing the bold claims in his opening. He almost acknowledged that his prescriptions were of far smaller scope than his diagnosis at the essay's start.[6] We now attend to his opening and closing in detail.

At essay's start Orwell posited that reciprocal political and linguistic decline followed from "political and economic causes" that he neither explored nor seemed to regard as controversial. Indeed, he seems to have presumed that some "general collapse"[7] of British civilization had set English politics and the English language to worsening each other. He did not explore how such a general collapse led to specific, poor habits of either politics or prose. He did not, that we two can detect, propose that anything could or should be done about this general collapse. Instead, he focused on reciprocating consequences of the general collapse: Decadent politics promulgates sloppy thinking that make English slovenly; slovenly language in turn enables foolish thoughts to prevail and to spread.[8]

By the last two paragraphs Orwell excused his third list of the essay, six feeble placebos that are the most often reproduced advice of the classic:

> These rules sound elementary, and so they are, but they demand a deep change of attitude in anyone who has grown used to writing in the style now fashionable. One could keep all of them and still write bad English, but one could not write the kind of stuff that I quoted in those five specimens at the beginning of this article.

Formulating six rules to prevent writers from creating such stuff as the five specimens that he quoted early in his essay seems a bit less adventuresome than decrying, as he did the first two paragraphs, the crises in politics and language.

Later in the book, we will embrace Orwell's advocacy of a change of attitude, so we do not contrast Orwell's minor cure-somes or cure-mosts (the six rules) to his systemic diagnosis to argue that his systemic fears should be disregarded or forgotten. Rather we stress that the essay declared "that one can probably bring about some improvement by starting at the verbal end" and [that] "one can at least change one's own habits, and from time to time one can even, if one jeers loudly enough, send some worn-out and useless phrase . . . into the dustbin, where it belongs," it provided feeble prescriptions to any readers who took seriously the claim that political and linguistic decay might be reversed. But we hope to provide a way to take Orwell's systemic thinking more seriously.

Orwell's Less Obvious Semantic Attitude—To take Orwell's representation of political communication seriously, we must abstract it from his essay. This we do in Table 3.2, which magnifies a column of our tabular overview in Table 3.1. We elaborate briefly on that tabular representation below:

The Dominant Content Row: **Linguistic swindles and perversions [Orwell's terms] displace concrete, clear, and candid expressions to the detriment of politicking and language as well as of truth, understanding, clarity, and sense.** In his dire pretext and throughout his essay, Orwell inventoried various shortcomings of writing that, he claimed, exemplified how politics and language were imperiling each other. What makes his inventory semantic, in our view, is that he defined the decline of language mostly as a matter of making bad, lazy, or cynical choices among words and figures of speech.

The Purveyors Row: **Élites, parties, and politicos dispense clichés, euphemisms, abstractions, lies, and blather that reduce critical intelligence and defend indefensible top-down (mis)rule.** Orwell attributed most of the peril, both to the polity and to the language, to the manner in which political powers shape political writers and political communication. The powerful and the wordsmiths they employ mask tyrannies behind

Table 3.2 Focusing on Orwell's Semantic Attitude

	Orwell's Semantic Attitude
Dominant Content	**LINGUISTIC SWINDLES AND PERVERSIONS** **displace** concrete, clear, and candid expressions to the detriment of politics and language as well as of truth, understanding, clarity, and sense.
Purveyors	**ÉLITES, PARTIES, AND POLITICOS** **dispense** clichés, euphemisms, abstractions, lies, and blather that reduce critical intelligence and defend indefensible top-down (mis)rule.
Conveyors	**POLITICAL WRITERS** **supplant** vivid, candid descriptions and observations with prefabricated phrases to suit the convenience, expedience, and thoughtlessness of writers as well as the designs of (mis)leaders.
Consumers	**READERS** [*we presume*] **accept** prefabricated phrases as soothing substitutes for concrete, harsh facts and **acquiesce** in élites' (mis)rule owing to misleading usages that numb readers' brains.

catchphrases, slogans, and lies crafted to reveal what the more powerful want the less powerful to think about and to conceal what the more powerful would like the less powerful not even to perceive.

The Conveyors Row: **Political writers supplant vivid, candid descriptions and observations with prefabricated phrases to suit the convenience, expedience, and thoughtlessness of writers as well as the designs of (mis)leaders.** Perhaps despairing of reforming inveterate liars and confidence men, Orwell directed his ire toward his fellow political writers, who supplanted vivid, candid, revealing descriptions with characterizations fashioned by operatives to suit the interests of élites and suited to the ease and mindlessness of writers more interested in filing copy than in what the copy says. Political writers arouse and calm their audiences as the content provided by purveyors dictates.

The Consumers Row: **Readers accept prefabricated phrases as soothing substitutes for concrete, harsh facts and acquiesce in élites' (mis) rule owing to misleading or masking usages that numb readers' brains.** As we have noted, Orwell wrote little for or about readers, the consumers of political writing, so in our table we have speculated about what he might have said or meant to say about them.[9] He did express the view that semantics and hackneyed phrasings anesthetized minds, so we are not stretching in that regard.

In our view Orwell presumed a top-down, two-step representation that explained deficient content by purveyors of that content (élites and their operatives) who concocted too much political folderol and by conveyors of that content (writers and journalists) who promulgated élite-friendly messages. We suspect but cannot be sure from the essay that he had in mind consumers of that content who were taken in by the purveyor-conveyor two-step. The processes from top to bottom (and almost never from bottom to top when the élite-friendly messaging works as designed) seem to us to make his attitude predominately semantic. Writers' clichés and euphemisms, question-begging, and sheer cloudy vagueness; writers' reliance on verbal false limbs, pretentious diction, moribund metaphors; and other "swindles and perversions" are means by which apologists, the educated and cultured authors of broadcasts and print, assist élites to mislead masses.

Thus, in his essay as in his novels published before and after the essay,[10] Orwell presumed that contemporary regimes pretended to popular rule as a means of exerting, preserving, and extending control of less powerful people by the more powerful people, who brandished the rhetoric and symbols of self-governance and liberty to camouflage and to rationalize their domination of the powerless. "Politics and the English Language" concerned subtler domination than his novels but similar abuses of language by political parties and partisans other than Communist or Fascist.[11] Far nimbler and perhaps far more perilous to self-rule, such parties subverted the will of the people and appropriated symbols of democracy using catchphrases, slogans, shibboleths, and other untruths. Parties' platforms, politicians' promises, and other policy nostrums that almost no one would label totalitarian or authoritarian relied on public relations and on trafficking in stereotypes, prejudices, beliefs, and half-conscious verities. To the readers of his novels, then, the top-down, two-step, "Semantic Attitude" seems characteristic of Orwell.

That seeming likeness may hide the perils of Orwell's overstressing semantics and understressing systems that he invoked at the beginning and end of his essay. Unlike the porcine élite who exploited semantics in *Animal Farm* and the inhuman élite who systematically and systemically commandeered language and thought in *1984*, Orwell's stenographers for political élites in "Politics and the English Language" oscillated between inept writing and lousy thinking that, he argued, mutually reinforced large-scale political and linguistic decay. The specimens of poor writing, far from endangering polity, language, or readers, at worst marred paragraphs. His cavalcade of cavils, we hope we are not too harsh to say, made for better T-shirts than systemic perversions.

We enumerate below five specimens[12] of Orwell's naïve semantics and systemic neglect to demonstrate that his most memorable contributions pertain mostly to phrasing and bear little on weightier matters with which he frames his essay. Having teased out his "macroscopic" representation of connections of politicking and language, we show how "microscopic" the bulk of his essay is by comparison.

[1] "If you simplify your English, you are freed from the worst follies of orthodoxy. You cannot speak any of the necessary dialects, and when you make a stupid remark its stupidity will be obvious, even to yourself."

In this specimen Orwell could scarcely have reduced problems of politicking and communication to the foibles of individual writers more and thereby understated more the systematic, systemic sanctioning of approved beliefs and prescribed actions. This oversimplification of the follies of orthodoxy parodies itself and trivializes his hifalutin pretense at the beginning and "lowerfalutin" end of the essay.[13] Much as we wish that realizing truth amid and against preaching were a matter of semantics, we insist that the worst follies of orthodoxy follow more from coercion, torture, deprivation, and other sanctions than from language that is not simple and straightforward enough.

[2] "Political language—and with variations this is true of all political parties, from Conservatives to Anarchists—is designed to make lies sound truthful and murder respectable, and to give an appearance of solidity to pure wind."

Orwell provides multiple T-shirts' worth of slogans in specimen two and stabs at partisanship in hard-hitting prose that is itself sloganeering. True, purveyors and conveyors craft accounts to disguise lies, to cover up crimes, and to parade blather as common sense. However, his exposure of Machiavellian designs overlooks modern myths and rituals that routinely make lying unnecessary or impossible, murder justifiable or heroic, and pure wind a ritualistic or idealistic breath of fresh air. Systems of beliefs and behaviors corrupt polities and languages wholesale in part **because** purveyors and conveyors distract critical thinkers with the retail politicking that he ridicules.

[3] "The great enemy of clear language is insincerity. When there is a gap between one's real and one's declared aims, one turns . . . to long words and exhausted idioms, like a cuttlefish spurting out ink."

A great enemy of clarity is insincerity, but many insincere and cynical pronouncements work because they consist of clear, concise, simple language. Orwell was right to urge individual political writers to clarity and candor in their scribbling. Beyond that homily his sentences were fatuous: Individual writers' clarity could never appreciably retard the destruction of English by authorities and authoritarians. Instead, he should have expected authorities and authoritarians to employ experts in public relations to disguise ulterior motives in simple, deceptively straightforward, mesmerizing slogans, words that succeed while policies fail.[14] Spurters of ink for whom (or at whom) he was writing did not create gaps between actual and apparent motives any more than they could redress gaps by dispersing semantic clouds spurted by élites and politicos.

[4]   "In our time it is broadly true that political writing is bad writing. Where it is not true, it will generally be found that the writer is some kind of rebel, expressing his private opinions and not a 'party line.' Orthodoxy, of whatever color, seems to demand a lifeless, imitative style."

In other words, good political writing tended to reject party lines in favor of rebellious candor, whereas poor political writing, Orwell presumed, systematically debilitated English to favor repetitive cant. The orthodoxies against which he inveighed in his writing and even in his employment at the BBC (The British Broadcasting Corporation), however, were scarcely renowned for dull slogans or images, so we cannot figure out what political writing he derided beyond the Communist pamphlet he decreed to be representative. A sentence from a left-wing tract might display a "lifeless, imitative style," but such fringe ranting cannot ground his generalization.[15]

[5]   "What is above all needed is to let the meaning choose the word, and not the other way around. In prose, the worst thing one can do with words is surrender to them. When you think of a concrete object, you think wordlessly, and then, if you want to describe the thing you have been visualizing you probably hunt about until you find the exact words that seem to fit it. When you think of something abstract you are more inclined to use words from the start, and unless you make a conscious effort to prevent it, the existing dialect will come rushing in and do the job for you, at the expense of blurring or even changing your meaning. Probably it is better to put off using words as long as possible and get one's meaning as clear as one can through pictures and sensations."

Orwell in specimen five supplies writers a stunning semantics. We do not mean "stunning" figuratively. We mean that to read specimen five slowly and carefully is to halt, retreat, reread, and then to sit paralyzed for moments trying to decide what to say about his theory of composition. His emphasis on the visual and the vivid, evident throughout the essay, is consistent with his recommendation of being as concrete as one can. Beyond that recommendation, his advice to writers is peculiar and almost perverse. Writers who put off using words as long as possible and dwell on images and impressions are delivering themselves and their words to those who shape images and who thereby manage impressions in modern polities. This is one way in which Orwell's advice is almost perversely misaligned with politics in 1945, 1984, or in 2018. More practically and less politically, many writers discover and sharpen what they want to express by writing or talking, not necessarily by thinking of images and then finding words in the manner he describes.

In these five "specimens" and elsewhere, Orwell's most substantial objection to writers' trafficking in hackneyed phrases and buzzwords is that such words and phrases camouflage tactically and cover strategically actions and decisions that otherwise would fail to secure popular approval. That systemic problem should interest many readers and writers. It certainly interests us. What Orwell did not see or admit, however, was that, relative to writers' hiding responsibility and power, writers' addiction to facile, hackneyed, labor-saving phrases usually mattered little.[16]

Beyond his most quotable sentiments, Orwell identifies four common missteps, prescribes six questions, and, more famously, propounds six rules for political writers, his explicit targets in the essay. What he identifies seems insufficient to deal with the mutually reinforcing spirals of politics and language. His list of four common missteps—dying metaphors; operators or verbal false limbs; pretentious diction; and meaningless words—scarcely seem up to the task of destroying politics and English. The six questions are not as purely semantic as the six rules, but neither questions nor rules amount to much more than a whine against reciprocating bad politicking and bad writing.

What we rehearse at such length above may be evident to most readers of the essay. We spelled it out because relating Orwell's particularized remedies to his overall diagnosis would provide the only way in which his essay might cohere. Further, we want to demonstrate how he misrepresented interrelations among the powerful, political communicators, and audiences. He supposed that the powerful and their agents swindled writers and perverted language by crafting phrases to cover "lies, evasions, folly, hatred, and schizophrenia"[17] to dupe the masses and simulate self-governance. Such phrases in turn make it far less costly or difficult for political writers to produce copy, so writers pass along the prefab phrases to audiences who would be taken in. Nefarious leaders, in sum, design a pageant that lazy, thoughtless writers script before credulous and sometimes deranged audiences. Political leaders rely on political writers to adjust the chains that keep readers watching images on the walls of Plato's cave.[18]

A memorable passage from "Politics and the English Language" drives home just how semantic and pre-textual Orwell's presumptions and representation were.

> In our time, political speech and writing are largely the defense of the indefensible. Things like the continuance of British rule in India, the Russian purges and deportations, the dropping of the atom bombs on Japan, can indeed be defended, but only by arguments which are too brutal for most people to face, and which do not square with the professed aims of the political parties. Thus political language has to consist largely of euphemism, question-begging and sheer cloudy vagueness. Defenseless villages are bombarded from the air, the inhabitants driven out into the countryside, the cattle machine-gunned, the huts set on fire with incendiary bullets: this is called *pacification*. Millions of peasants are robbed of their farms and sent trudging along the roads with no more than they can carry: this is called *transfer of population* or *rectification of frontiers*. People are imprisoned for years without trial, or shot in the back of the neck or sent to die of scurvy in Arctic lumber camps: this is called *elimination of unreliable elements*. Such phraseology is needed if one wants to name things without calling up mental pictures of them.

Orwell made his **semantic** attitude obvious in this passage. Yet his semantics undermined the realism or practicality of not just his essay as a whole but his point in the inset passage. If the demystifying attitude that he was striving to inculcate in writers led political critics to expose the euphemisms that he italicized, what politics-quashing, language-destroying regime would want for wordsmiths to conjure substitute euphemisms? If the feeble remedies that he produced by essay's end were to succeed, would miseries and injustices thereby be ameliorated, or would mental pictures[19] be screened behind other words? What is worse, he wrote on the cusp of television's rise. Until nearly the end of Orwell's days, movies and newsreels were the major sources of moving pictures other than mental. Newspaper photographers sometimes fed mental images with snapshots, but seldom the disturbing images or sequences that TV would make routine. Radio broadcasts conjured mental images, but visualizations varied with the proclivities and talents of audiences at least as much as with the dispatches of correspondents. The more chilling the misery that viewers might see, the more non-euphemizing words speakers and writers would have to supply to overcome the raw materials that purveyors and conveyors would spin.

Some readers recall "Politics and the English Language" so fondly that they are ill-disposed to notice that Orwell at the end of his essay offers mild if not timid if not silly rules that stand little chance of redressing or even addressing the bold diagnosis of systemic decline from which he started. His large-scale diagnosis is readily seen as merest pretext if one reads the last paragraph of "Politics and the English Language" with the first two paragraphs in mind. Little wonder "Orwellian" is so often used for semi-transparent semantic dodges.[20] Pretext aside, "Politics and the English Language" collates various gripes and complaints alongside but not in any strong relation to a conception of politics and language either haphazard or convenient or both.

Our Responsibilities in Assigning "Politics and the English Language"

We cannot believe we assigned this essay to our students so blithely. We upbraid ourselves for failing to guide those student-readers properly as we offer Table 3.3, which distinguishes between the problems on which Orwell's semantic attitude focused and those on which Jacques Ellul, superb theorist of propaganda, focused with a systemic attitude.

To assuage our guilt at having assisted our students so meagerly, we must save Orwell's contributions from—irony of ironies—what Orwell writes. Earlier we argued that Orwell's macro case was nonsense when he wrote it and when *Horizon* and *The New Republic* published it but that it has become ever more pertinent to politicking and communicating. Before we can establish his large-scale, 21st-century pertinence—alas!—we must establish his large-scale, 20th-century impertinence. To that task we now turn, fleshing out what appears in the table.

Section Two—Orwell's Semantic Attitude, Ellul's Systematic Attitude?

Orwell's implicit Semantic Attitude misapprehended interrelations of élites, politicos, and writers and only inferentially considered readers. By contrast, Jacques Ellul offered at about the same time[21] a systematic attitude that portrayed top-down communications which ruled modern polities through orchestrated, totally suffusing deployment of mass media all while maintaining appearances of bottom-up politicking and governing. Ellul's more systematic understanding of apparently but minimally bottom-up alongside latently but overwhelmingly top-down political communication emphasized the encompassing management of the wants and needs of targets of such communication—the consumers of mass media whom Orwell neglected.

To contrast the prominent role of consumers in Ellul's representation of the communications system with the minuscule role of readers in Orwell's

Table 3.3 Orwell's Semantic versus Ellul's Systematic Attitude

	Orwell's Semantic Attitude		Ellul's Systematic Attitude
Dominant Content	**LINGUISTIC SWINDLES AND PERVERSIONS** **displace** concrete, clear, and candid expressions to the detriment of politicking and language as well as of truth, understanding, clarity, and sense.	→	**ORCHESTRATED ORTHODOXY AND ORTHOPRAXY** **surround** audiences with multimedia messages and images that reinforce one another, that arouse and calm by turns, and that conform masses' actions and beliefs to regimes' designs and legitimation.
Purveyors	**ÉLITES, PARTIES, AND POLITICOS** **dispense** clichés, euphemisms, abstractions, lies, and blather that reduce critical intelligence and defend indefensible top-down (mis)rule.	→	**ÉLITES AND PROPAGANDISTS** **choreograph** verifiable or at least not disprovable information, misinformation, and disinformation to legitimize top-down rule as if it issued from bottom-up consent.
Conveyors	**POLITICAL WRITERS** **supplant** vivid, candid descriptions and observations with prefabricated phrases to suit the convenience, expedience, and thoughtlessness of writers as well as the designs of (mis)leaders.	→	**MASS MEDIA** **transform** communication through images, immediacy, and abstractions that disengage critical faculties, incite actions, and create needs, expectations, and satisfactions.
Consumers	**READERS** [*we presume*] **accept** prefabricated phrases as soothing substitutes for concrete, harsh facts and **acquiesce** in élites' (mis)rule owing to misleading usages that numb readers' brains.	→	**CURRENT-EVENTS MAVENS** **need** and expect current, credible stories and imagery to make them appear critical and intelligent consumers of information and shapers if not makers of important decisions in the polity.

semantic catalogue of verbal subterfuges, we explore Ellul's representation from the bottom row ("Consumers") of Table 3.3 up. We find Ellul's descriptions more realistic, more systematic, and more concrete than those of that apostle of the concrete, Eric Arthur Blair.

The Consumers Row: **"Current Events Mavens"**[22] **need and expect current, credible stories and imagery to make mavens appear critical and intelligent consumers of information and shapers if not makers of important decisions in the polity.** In place of Orwell's readers who, we presume because Orwell does not state, accept soothing, vacuous, familiar phrases and acquiesce in top-down rule, we derive from Ellul consumers of systematically orchestrated and utterly surrounding mass communication who seek and expect stories and imagery that make these consumers seem critical, smart, and involved even as those mass communications make consumers less critical, more credulous and less savvy, and less involved. These "Current Events Mavens" crave what news media and entertainment media provide: words and images that appeal to tastes that consumers have acquired over years of reading papers, listening to radio, and watching television. Far from the dull, lifeless prose that he associated with orthodoxy, the "infotainment"[23] that Current Events Mavens crave suffuses radio, newsreels, films, and photographs with narratives and images. Dramaturgy and diversions far more vivid than any political writer would be likely to produce attract patronage and hunger for news on which modern news media and infotainment depend. This in turn rewards news media and politicos for spreading infotainment. Ellul, in sum, described more realistically and more concretely the mass-mediated readers, listeners, and viewers whom Orwell almost entirely overlooked beyond the pundits and professors against whom and about which he wrote.[24] Dwelling on how political writers mangled language, he little considered how Current Events Mavens who made up the audiences for much political writing might shape and be shaped by political writing.

The Conveyors Row: **Mass media transform communication through images, immediacy, and abstractions that disengage critical faculties, incite actions, and create needs, expectations, and satisfactions.** Orwell presumed that expedient, thoughtless, and prefabricated phrases doom politics and language, but Ellul took a more realistic and concrete view about how mass media, and not merely political writers, conveyed political messages. Conveying media, attuned to marketing, competition, and the tastes and expectations that Current-Events Mavens acquired from media and socialization, reinforce emphasis on vivid or lurid infotainment. Tabloids and other print media conditioned consumers to titillation during Orwell's life; broadcast and electronic media have encompassed the post-Orwell globe with news that amuses or scares. News media especially condition consumers to titillation and other "news values" until those values come to define news and mavens come to expect or demand entertaining diversions. Among the pernicious consequences of news media's competing to entertain as well as inform is the tendency to "normalize."[25] Mainstream norms shape what media regard as news, what reporters and editors recognize and understand enough to report quickly and comprehensibly (rather than comprehensively), and what audiences are likely to find accessible and satisfying. The dominant content of the news and of political writing based on the news likewise must begin and largely stay within the "channels" of common norms.

The Purveyors Row: **Élites and their propagandists organize verifiable or at least not disprovable information, misinformation, and disinformation to legitimize top-down rule as if it issued from bottom-up consent.** The longer that the Current-Events Mavens and the news media that feed them have trained one another, the more that purveyors have learned to tailor their propaganda to expectations and appetites. Such a media loop is more pertinent than the loop Orwell conjured.[26] In place of élites and politicos who dispense lies, abstractions, euphemisms, and other reassuring messages, Ellul supposed that opinion leaders orchestrated expressions of beliefs and choreographed expressive actions through mass-mediated messages systematically crafted and widely disseminated. Ellul's conception of how opinion leaders lead mass opinion turned attention from political writers who uncritically conveyed prefabricated phrases and legitimizing euphemisms to how propagandists used mass media to transform messages and to convey imagery, immediacy, and "infotainment" that a) made critical thinking ever less likely; b) legitimized élite decisions and practices even as they delegitimized alternatives; and c) encouraged appetites, expectations, and satisfactions that political writers of Orwell's persuasion could not imagine or emulate.

The Dominant Content Row: **Orchestrated orthodoxy and orthopraxy surround audiences with multimedia messages and images that reinforce one another, that arouse and calm by turns, and that unify the actions and beliefs to regimes' designs and legitimation.** Having quoted one of Orwell's best "T-shirt" lines above—"Political language . . . is designed to make lies sound truthful and murder respectable, and to give an appearance of solidity to pure wind"—we now identify another key difference between Orwell and Ellul. Ellul argued that, far from Orwell's semantic tricks that disguised lies, the most effective political communications build on truth as much and as often as possible. Ellul argued that the dominant content of modern polities was not—at least until the 21st century—élite-serving lies masked by semantic subterfuges and tall tales, but truths, statistics, and stories that propagandists interpreted in service of their causes and ends.

From the bottom of Table 3.3 to its top, then, Ellul's systemic under-standing of top-down, multi-step manipulation of attitudes contrasts sharply with how Orwell's fussing over words, phrases, and images directed atten-tion toward trivial problems with the composition and editing of political writing and, more important, away from coordinated, inundating ortho-doxy. Orwell misstated the very orthodoxy against which he inveighed and thereby obscured forces that eroded politics and language much more than mixed metaphors, clumsy euphemisms, or cloudy vagueness could. Effec-tive political communications conform beliefs, attitudes, opinions, and val-ues to systems of mutually reinforcing or coevolving truths that purport to serve recipients of messages but tend to serve purveying élites and convey-ing media far better far more often.

In ascending order of importance, let us now recap three advantages of Ellul's systemic approach over Orwell's semantics. First, Ellul's concept of the Current Events Maven better accounts for euphemisms, clichés, and other swindles and perversions than Orwell's pretext(s) do. To ruin a lan-guage and a polity, writers must deploy swindles, perversions, tropes, and banter suited to securing credence and actions or inactions premised on belief. Ellul stressed that effective shaping of attitudes and thus of citizenry demanded the eliciting of assent or at least acquiescence and the reinforce-ment of assent or acquiescence through acts or choices that gave target audi-ences a stake in continuing to accept or to acquiesce. Orwell went with semantics; Ellul opted for conditioning of minds and actions.

More important is Ellul's insight that modern propaganda inculcates appetites for and expectations of more propaganda and further propagandiz-ing. Effective 20th-century propaganda systems tailor what they propagate **less** to the cheap euphemisms and trite talking points against which Orwell inveighed and **more** to the sociological and psychological conditions and processes of a mass polity. Ellul showed how modern propaganda created artificial needs that served propagandists much better than propagandees and that altered members of the polity psychologically and sociopolitically to suit propagandees to propaganda.

Ellul's third and most important contribution: Modern, systematic pro-paganda consists less in lies and tall tales than in truth fiendishly adhered to. Fashionable as it was for Orwell to emphasize dodgy semantics that obscured lies and mere wind, and audacious as it was for him to characterize politics as "lies, evasions, folly, hatred, and schizophrenia,"[27] Ellul taught us that propagandists anticipate every truth that could undermine messages or obstruct ongoing relations with targets and subjects, and then reinterpret such truth to correspond with or at least not contradict propaganda.

In sum, if we recondition Orwell's diagnosis to suit modern political systems (politics) more and fuss about semantics (language) less, we may focus on his greatest contribution to our understanding politics and the English language. Orwell's semantic diagnosis does not much fit political practice in the middle of the 20th century, especially in the light of Ellul's systematic diagnosis of modern propaganda states that relied on as much truth as they could muster and assiduously avoided flat-out mendacity if they could. He did not show that linguistic swindles and perversions— lies, vacuities, evasions, ambiguities, folly, euphemisms, hatred, mere wind, and schizophrenia—were on the rise in 1945–46; rather, he merely asserted such from his first sentence.[28] Ellul theorized why lies, vacuities, ambiguities, euphemisms, and mere wind (if not Orwell's swindles and perversions) were, if changed at all, on the decline after WWII: Totalizing, suffusing, engulfing strategies and tactics relied on the verifiable as much as practicable, and then on what could not be disproved as much as propagandists could manage. More important, Ellul showed why levels of puffery and pettifoggery mattered little amid all-embracing systems of belief and action suited to top-down control and management of truth. Orwell's semantic nostrums might treat annoying symptoms but could neither halt nor reverse system-wide decadence, but that mattered little because his attitude was more truculent defamation than credible diagnosis.[29] His attitude was pretext if not pretense, an alarum by which to pull readers into his essay and an extravagant frame by which to suggest that his essay was more than grumbles and objections that had accumulated in Orwell's notebooks. The foregoing, at any rate, is what we believe we have established thus far this chapter.

Section Three—Orwell's Greatest Hit . . . of the Truthy 21st Century

However, what once was pretext now is pertinent, maybe even prescient, so readers now should regard Orwell's diagnosis seriously. Nowadays politics in general and political writing in particular depend ever more on lies and lying, on swindles of citizenry and perversions of phrases, and on euphemisms and other wind. In the late 20th century and early 21st century, the system we have earlier named pseudocracy resembles greatly the republic of mendacity and pettifoggery that he prematurely presumed.

To concede the ubiquity of falsehoods in present-day American politicking, for example, establishes anew why Orwell's catalogue of swindles and perversions and his lists of questions and rules are each and all beside the larger point with which he framed his essay. That concession requires recognition of pseudocracy, a rule of and by falsehoods that is a 21st-century American manifestation of the political decline in Britain about which he wrote.[30] A system that runs on falsehoods encourages deliberate or thoughtless deceit both by rewarding deceivers and by legitimizing deceptions until dishonesty becomes normal. The falsehoods that rule the polity and the lingo are neither the hackneyed, ad hoc "swindles and perversions" that Orwell ascribed to writers nor the system-saturating orthodoxy and orthopraxy that Ellul described. Rather, pseudocracy runs on visions and versions tailored to and by **factions**.

Pseudocracy stands for a system in which falsehoods or deceptions routinely prevail over truths or candor. Our coinage uses "pseudo-" to label the range from flat-out lies to strategic and tactical feints to "wedge-issues" and impression-management and all the way to "dog-whistle" appeals to racism, White Supremacy, misogyny, xenophobia, homophobia, and science-denial. Our coinage uses "-cracy" to comprise the range from sway and suasion to power and force. Pseudocracy denotes a system in which falsehoods have proliferated means by which politicos and others may seem to be what they cannot be. Political and linguistic artifice lies in seeming not untruthful while expressing words or sentiments far more useful than true. As pseudocrats stretch their truths further and further from honesty and truthfulness, they exaggerate whatever distance remains between their practices and manifest mendacity. The pseudocratic polity has so defined dishonesty downward that it suggests the blackguard whom Yeats lampooned as "one [w]ho, were it proved he lies, [w]ere neither shamed in his own [n]or in his neighbours' eyes."[31]

In his campaign and presidency, Donald J. Trump has recently practiced and exacerbated the foregoing conception of the pseudocracy so that "truth" has been fragmented into manifold truthiness.[32] (Trump is of course not the only one to embody pseudocracy, only one of the most grotesque, narcissistic, and dangerous to do so.) This truthiness provides what pundits or other purveyors want others to concede the facts to be, as opposed to what purveyors know or suspect or fear the facts might be. When demonstrable truth will not serve a cause as well as arguable truths, purveyors resort to truthiness.

The truthiness that Donald Trump has prosecuted differs greatly from the obdurate, unifying, abiding, concrete truth that Orwell feared political writers were obscuring with their hackneyed tropes and blowsy abstractions and from the verifiable, demonstrable truth that Ellul argued propagandists commandeered and contextualized and interpreted and repackaged and matched to action. Niches, cliques, factions, and other "silos" craft their own truths to suit their designs, values, preferences, and then disseminate these truths through mass media dedicated to the groups' visions and to the cultivation of in-group beliefs and actions.

Trump's successes demonstrate that in our "post-fact" society we cannot count on intractable facts or agreed-upon facts. Orwell and Ellul lived in an age when people were entitled to their own opinions but not to their own facts. Trump and we live in an era when we each are entitled to our own opinions as well as to "facts" [and "alternative facts"] suited to those opinions. Trump has updated Orwell's semantics and Ellul's propaganda systems to suit burgeoning pseudocracy.

We summarize Trump's practices in Table 3.4. We proceed from the truthy content that dominates our politics and language after the demise of singular Truth and of consensual, common facts. Then we show how truthiness conditions purveyors, conveyors, and consumers. Thus, we attribute to "Dominant Content" importance beyond its topmost position in Table 3.4. We take Trump to portend that, more than Orwell's writers [Conveyors] or Ellul's propagandists [Purveyors], truthiness [Dominant Content] shapes and degrades 21st-century politics and language.[33]

The Dominant Content Row: **Customized versions of reality conform perceptions and interpretations to polarized, prefabricated viewpoints that cohere in mass media, groupthink, and echo chambers to fragment factuality.** Fragmented, factionalized truths, once formulated, persist and evolve in tensions between holding adherents and mobilizing converts. Long before "post-fact" blared from broadcasts during the 2016 campaigns, Farhad Manjoo noted increasing mendacity in the politics and language of 21st-century America.[34] As truthiness escalates, tangled webs of material interests, symbolic suspicions, inter-group contentions, intra-group surmises, and what the political market will bear, buy, or believe shape factions at least as much as leaders of factions shape them. While Orwell decried linguistic swindles

Table 3.4 Trump's Truthy Politics and Language

Trump's Truthy Aptitude 2015–17
CUSTOMIZED VERSIONS OF REALITY **conform perceptions and interpretations to polarized, prefabricated viewpoints that cohere in mass media, groupthink, and echo chambers to fragment factuality.**
CLIQUES AND FACTIONS **disseminate truths adapted from and to their group realities through disparate media to "authenticate" realities or to make realities arguably populist or both.**
SPINNERS AND CASUISTS **coevolve truths and groups through tested, tailored slogans and shows that harden cleavages and affirm truth-holders while they defame truth-rejecters.**
TRUE BELIEVERS **need and expect "new" reports to reinforce set identities, cleavages, and views of in-group and to refute images, issues, and views of opponents as counterfactual.**

and perversions **of political writers** (whom we call the conveyors) for hiding intractable truths and enabling politicos' undetectable falsehoods to distort actuality; and Ellul observed how **propagandists** (purveyors) orchestrated beliefs and actions to incorporate undeniable truths into accommodations of actuality; Trump shows how **the visions and versions** of factions supplant actuality. To an extent, then, the dominant content of our politics shapes purveyors and conveyors much more than actuality directs them. Orwell's swindles and perversions abide and abound, and Ellul's orthodoxy and orthopraxy persist, but politics today also features prefabricated visions that disseminators ought to or do know are false and polarized versions of reality that condition the perceptions and interpretations of individuals centrifugally. These visions and versions sharply diverge from mainstream consensus or common sense. Centripetally visions and versions coalesce in systems of groupthink that envelop purveyors and conveyors alike in truthy certainty.[35]

The Purveyors Row: **Cliques and factions disseminate truths adapted from and to their group realities through disparate media to "authenticate" realities or to make realities arguably populist or both.** Although even truthy factions express themselves concretely, clearly, and candidly when such expressions serve their interests, advantages, or public relations, they market factional views more abstractly or symbolically, more ambiguously or vaguely, and more tactically or strategically as keeping their stories straight and their contentions at least modestly plausible dictate. Purveyors formulate talking points that are not quite true and not quite false but that serve factional narratives. If factions, pundits, or other politicos find such talking points potentially helpful or profitable, the talking points not only spread quickly but also echo across the polity. Even truthier, purveyors craft pronouncements that are true in approximately one sense yet misleading in meanings that, purveyors know, audiences most likely apply.[36] Clever, careful phrasing has profited leaders and their supporters always, but modern factions test talking points before focus groups and pay wordsmiths to evade or to supplant truth.[37] Factions tailor perceptions to in-group interpretations and constructions with far more regard for credence than veracity. Through such large-scale designs and situation-specific messages, factions purvey truthy mendacity while charging opponents and infidels with deceits and diversions.

The Conveyors Row: **Spinners and casuists in mass media coevolve truths and groups through tested, tailored slogans and shows that harden cleavages and affirm truth-holders even while they defame truth-rejecters.** Whatever purveyors concoct, the suffusing media must communicate for factional truths to affect politics, in so doing excluding solid information. Orwell targeted political writers as important communicators, and Ellul attended to those who coordinated mass media as conveyors, but pseudocracy requires spinners and casuists to spew talking points.[38] By spinners and casuists we mean what in modern U.S. politics are called "the chattering classes:" pundits, editorialists, commentators, experts, celebrities, pollsters, consultants, and public intellectuals who are well positioned to be quoted or paraphrased throughout mass media.[39] Beyond Sunday talk shows, panels on 24/7 news networks, and shows that mix jokes or skits with almost-serious interviews, newer news media provide echo chambers in which purveyors repeat factional truths and refute counter-truths and conventional beliefs.[40] Thus mass-mediated cocoons of truthiness insulate or isolate members of factions from information or perspectives that might disconfirm factional truths.

The Consumers Row: **True believers**[41] **need and expect "new" reports to reinforce set identities, cleavages, and views of in-group and to refute images, issues, and views of opponents as counterfactual.** We grant Orwell that ingenuous readers are easily taken in by euphemisms and other swindles and Ellul that current-events mavens long for approved topics for conversations, but Trump's campaigning as candidate and as President takes an additional step to represent consumers as true believers subject to sociological and psychological pressures to perceive and to conceive politics to suit their factions, to refute opponents, and to turn opponents into enemies. True, these consumers revel in talking points and other ready-made phrases, especially swindles and perversions that make them and their allies seem savvy. However, they value even more ready-made "truths" that make them "in the know" and those outside the faction in the dark. These consumers welcome new reports that confirm the rightness and rectitude of beliefs they have long or short held. However, they greet even more fresh fodder for colloquy to establish what the mainstream does not get and what conventional wisdom does not understand.[42] Factions and their truths "close the circle" for consumers, who thrive on the closure and certainty.

In sum, we take the successes of Trump to suggest that niches, cliques, and other groups—we slyly label them factions—have fragmented shared truths into distinctive truths that better suit the designs, values, and preferences of factions. Purveyors working inside or alongside these factions disseminate these truths through narrowcast media dedicated to factions' delusions, beliefs, and actions. Conveyors outside factions relay conflict and controversy with little attention to veracity beyond sourcing. Dissemination of truths through mass media recruits converts to factions, but that may not be truthy factions' primary activity, which is probably to perpetuate their groups and perspectives.

Orwell's characterization of the dominant content of politicking applies well to 21st-century politics and usage. Swindles and perversions abound, but they are less the conventional, convenient expressions that he presumes than calculated imaging and "messaging" with which he was not afflicted. Insincerity is still a great cause of unclear, misleading expression, but the techniques of the 21st century have remade insincerity into a science of scams. Lies and insincerity that he dismissed as thoughtless blather have become thoughtful design. More important, political scammers and confidence artists in the 21st century have broken the total, integrated system of propagandizing about which Ellul wrote down into images and beliefs so personalized that the identification and integration of recruits to factions has rendered members of factions almost immune to appeals to a shared world of facts or factuality. In 21st-century pseudocracy, factional falsehoods rule, cult-like factions proliferate, and facts fade.

Given that the content of 21st-century politicking so resembles Orwell's trenchant critique, it cannot surprise us that purveyors of that content are less the haphazard liars whose clichés, euphemisms, and other semantic perversions Orwell excoriated than they are systematic, almost scientific panderers. He could not have imagined how imagery and broadcast media would transmogrify politics, especially in the United States. Nonetheless, his description of and disgust with élites, politicos, and especially political writers who habitually abused language to reduce critical intelligence and to defend indefensible top-down (mis)rule seems spot on. He aptly described an outcome but missed the processes that would lead to it.

He was dashing off an essay in which he embedded some peeves, so he presumed a rigid dichotomy between those who trafficked in "lies, evasions, folly, hatred, and schizophrenia" and truth-seekers and truth-tellers. Political writers should stop assisting the former group and aid instead the sincere and the candid, Orwell opined. Looking back more than 70 years after he wrote and writing at a considerably more leisurely pace, we represent politics and language via a hub of what is absolutely, resolutely verifiable and undeniable from which extend in multiple directions "spokes" of what is not absolutely, resolutely, demonstrably a deliberate lie. Political spokespersons operate along "spokes" of what is neither demonstrably true nor demonstrably a deliberate deception. Politicos push opponents' characterizations and communication away from centripetal truth and as far toward absolute mendacity as consumers might believe; meanwhile, politicos liken characterizations and communications that issue from politicos' own factions to absolute or at least relative truth(s). Opponents purvey untruths as allies speak or write truths.[43] Such characterizations oversimplify when they do not defame, so declaring that "they" lie while "we" tell the truth may be commonplace instances of "making stuff up." We presume a multiplicity of ways in which politicos and citizens may avoid telling the truth or accuse opponents of dishonesty rather than error, of deception rather than misunderstanding, and so on. We further presume that resembling or dissembling truth is a matter of degrees. From every hub of "absolute" truth we imagine, then, we might imagine one or more spokes of relative truths and falsehoods, each continuum extending toward an absolute falsehood and deliberate deception that will almost never be reached or admitted.[44] These spokes allow proliferations of alternatives to telling the truth that can be differentiated from absolute deceit, although neither absolute truthfulness nor absolute mendacity need be out of play.[45]

"Stretching the truth," then, is a gradual but imposing way in which to extend the range of what counts as honesty or at least what does not count as rank dishonesty. All participants in politics proclaim truthfulness as an ideal but then distance some spin, euphemisms, doubletalk, and other deceptions from absolute mendacity so that what is not true will appear relatively true or almost true rather than merely not perfectly false. When people stretch the truth, they define dishonesty "outward."[46]

The "pseudo-" in "pseudocracy," on our presumptions, may stand for any number of expressions, acts, or practices that fall short of or rise above standards for either lying or truth-telling. Honest mistakes may be negligibly different from inadvertent truth-telling. Reckless untruths and thoughtless verities may be placed further from dedicated truth-telling. For many or most political observers or participants, spin and other interpretive arts by which truths are fabricated or exaggerated to hide inconvenient truths or perilous untruths are not quite lies. The spokes represent more than one scale in more than one plane along which to array descriptions of expressions, acts, or character flaws. For example, the scale used in barrooms, in our experience, is very different from the scale used in courtrooms. Tall tales and self-aggrandizing sagas in casual settings may carry the narrator far from truth or truthfulness, whereas deviations from "the truth, the whole truth, and nothing but the truth" may carry a witness far toward a jail cell.[47]

Need we add that the middle range between honesty and dishonesty varies by the perspective of the political observer or participant? If **my** candidate or our party frightens or threatens a group with tales of what opponents may be up to, the candidate or the party are not "just making stuff up" but may be exaggerating for impact and advantage. However, if **their** candidate or their party deploys hyperbole, **our** side will push such exaggerations toward dishonesty or mendacity, all the while claiming to be observing rather than constructing. I and they will likely press our position sincerely. Pitched battles to label "them" as habitual liars while defending "us" as occasionally overreaching (solely to vindicate some important truth, of course) are thus a predictable feature of spectra between telling the truth as best we can and various forms of error or dishonesty. Moreover, by inducing us to identify with "my" or "their" alleged views, pseudocrats addict us to pseudocracy. Partisanship is a gateway drug to pseudocracy.

Trump's Factional Truthiness Aptitude corresponds to and explains the large-scale diagnosis from which Orwell begins his essay far better than Orwell's Semantic Attitude. If Trump's rampant truthiness resembles the malady that Orwell used as a pretext for his gripes and jibes, then the relevance of his main claim obtains, so that our task is to recontextualize the essay. Then readers in general and especially our students can see how a 1945–46 essay applies to readers' and students' present.

Table 3.5 Orwell's Semantic Attitude and Trump's Truthy Aptitude

	Orwell's Semantic Attitude (1945–46)		Trump's Truthy Aptitude (2015–17)
Dominant Content	LINGUISTIC SWINDLES AND PERVERSIONS **displace** concrete, clear, and candid expressions to the detriment of politicking and language as well as of truth, understanding, clarity, and sense.	→	CUSTOMIZED VERSIONS OF REALITY **conform** perceptions and interpretations to polarized, prefabricated viewpoints that cater to echo chambers that splinter factuality.
Purveyors	ÉLITES, PARTIES, AND POLITICOS **dispense** clichés, euphemisms, abstractions, lies, and blather that reduce critical intelligence and defend indefensible top-down (mis)rule.	→	NICHES, CLIQUES, FACTIONS **disseminate** truths adapted from and to their group realities through disparate media to authenticate or to make arguable.
Conveyors	POLITICAL WRITERS **supplant** vivid, candid descriptions and observations with prefabricated phrases to suit the convenience, expedience, and thoughtlessness of writers as well as the designs of (mis)leaders.	→	SPINNERS AND CASUISTS **coevolve** truths and groups through tested, tailored slogans and shows that harden cleavages and affirm truth-holders while they defame truth-rejecters.
Consumers	READERS [we presume] **accept** prefabricated phrases as soothing substitutes for concrete, harsh facts and **acquiesce** in élites' (mis)rule owing to misleading or masking usages that numb readers' brains.	→	TRUE BELIEVERS **need and expect** "new" reports to reinforce set identities, cleavages, and views of in-group and to refute images, issues, and views of opponents as counterfactual.

Section Four—Practices by Which Readers and Instructors Might Acquire Attitudes and Train Aptitudes to Overcome Irony One

The "change in attitude" about which Orwell spoke at the end of his essay may prove a suitable remedy for his diagnosis of mendacity and political decline, but only if writers and readers alike adopt his attitude and only if consumers of political communication acquire his aptitude for seeing through pseudocracy. Rather than to imagine that fastidious semantics can deflect politics and the English language from their dual duel to our death, writers and especially 21st-century readers must read him for **attitudes** that may with practice improve **aptitudes**.

Obviously, changed attitudes and acquired aptitudes will neither resolve nor reverse the decadence and pseudocracy that we have sketched. We offer no panaceas in place of Orwell's palliatives. Rather, before we conclude Chapter 3, we aim to reestablish a pertinence in the overall design of his essay. The large-scale diagnosis and small-bore remedies of "Politics and the English Language" were in 1945–46 mismatched. We cannot make his rules all that relevant to the even worse decay in politicking and usage that has put American English in an even worse way than the foibles and fumbles Orwell highlighted. In this section we try to resurrect the pertinence as we overcome the pedantry of his essay.

Orwell exhorted writers to change their attitudes, but writers likely will change only if audiences, campaigns, and economics reward or reinforce such changes. This means that the contents, purveyors, conveyors, and consumers in our tables above—and their predominate interrelations—must be addressed even though we cannot transform them. We see considerable potential in the essay for halting steps toward addressing contents, purveyors, conveyors, and consumers, but only by supplanting his pedanticism and prejudices with his far more useful attitudes and aptitudes.[48]

Attitudes and aptitudes will depend largely on technologies that emerged long after 1946 because the Internet, Comedy Central, Twitter, and similar deconstructing "New Media" promise instrumentalities by which Orwell's diagnoses might be remedied. Technological transformation—we curmudgeons cannot be sure they are net "advances"—may permit aptitude to grow from Orwell's attitude. We merely describe a short list of emergent technologies that might ameliorate truthiness and mendacity much better than fussing over swindles, perversions, or the passive voice. We begin with fisking.

New Media,[49] among other services, facilitate fisking, "going through a piece of writing line by line and arguing with it."[50] We use "fisking" to include paragraph-by-paragraph, passage-by-passage, and line-by-line arguing. A habit of fisking imbues readers with Orwellian skepticism and other attitudes even as it cultivates readers' aptitude for alertly engaging claims published and publicized. An alacrity for energetic, even contrarian reception of communication trains consumers to resist blandishments, flattery, and other tools of pseudocracy.

Most conventional media, printed or broadcast, could never afford the space in which to fisk even the most substantial published views. The Internet, by contrast, can afford the electrons. The fragmentation of our pseudocracy permits those with specialized interests and acumen to attend to detailed line-by-line or paragraph-by-paragraph refutations and leave the rest of the Internet to other pursuits. Fisking may not serve as a mass medium in every sense of "mass," for audiences for fisking will likely be even smaller and more factionalized than most audiences for most media. Fisking does serve, however, to lampoon and to expose the insincerity, deviousness, pretentiousness, and other ills for which Orwell prescribed semantic Band-Aids. Moreover, fisking's refutations or ridicule center on more substantial, consequential contentions than those at issue in his essay. Professor Laski's binge of double-negatives[51] or Dr. Hogben's semantic tangle[52] was never going to imperil the freedom of expression about which Dr. Laski wrote or the artificial language that Mr. Orwell did not tell readers that Professor Hogben was inventing. No one fisking, we hope, could be bothered with imperfections unrelated to misleading or misinforming readers.

Joan Walsh at *Salon* recently demonstrated a more conventional version of fisking.[53] Charles Murray stated, "In all the critiques of The Bell Curve in particular and my work more generally, no one ever accompanies their charges with direct quotes of what I've actually said. There's a reason for that." Ms. Walsh responded vehemently:

> That's absolute bullshit. For one thing, I've written about Murray's work extensively, and with lavish documentation and direct quotes (and I'm not the only one). Since I debated Murray on WBUR in 2012, I know he knows my work. So he's a liar when he says "no one ever accompanies their charges with direct quotes of what I've actually said." You can trust the rest of his self-defense as much as you can trust that last self-serving statement—which means not at all.

Ms. Walsh's retort, multiplied across media old and especially new by debunkers left and right, might scare some pseudocrats, perhaps even Dr. Murray, out of some misleading or mendacious statements.

Such fisking will not abolish ideology masquerading as science but will do more than quibbling about exhibits in Orwell's catalogue of swindles and perversions. Especially if more and more readers and viewers can be induced to adopt the common law maxim that a witness who testifies falsely in one matter may be distrusted in other matters to which the witness testifies, skeptical attitudes and debunking aptitudes may become habitual in U.S. politicking and governing.[54]

We now turn from fisking to aggregating. News-aggregating sites feature deconstructions amid amalgamated content, albeit separating reliable from unreliable content may challenge readers.[55] Fark.com, for example, not only accumulates reports from around media new and old but promotes comments on such news. Such sites sometimes deconstruct spin and mendacity as well as the other insincerity and blather about which Orwell so lathered himself. News aggregators imperil consumers, to be sure. The lure of lurid rumors and the joy of spreading reports that a consumer is first in some small circle to learn may make consumers complicit in misinformation. Still, routine exposure to the prevalence of misinformation alongside routine exposure of disinformation promises to wise up [and, alas, to wizen] consumers who, with enough practice, can cultivate an aptitude for opposing and maybe even reversing some truthy badinage, but such consumers must train themselves to counteract credulity and passivity.

Checking the pundits can supplement fisking and aggregating. Far more important than Orwell's discovering cant in a Communist pamphlet or blather in a letter to a newspaper, "pundit audits"[56] detect or construct bias in other media new and old.[57] Such websites as "Crooks and Liars" and "NewsBusters"[58] realize Orwellian attitude and hone anti-pseudocratic attitude. Even passive consumption of sites and skeptics who debunk nonsense may train consumers to be as skeptical as Orwell, which in turn may spur consumers to value sources that tend to reliable, factual information and to devalue sources that tend to untrustworthy, fatuous entertainment. Thus might consumers increase the ratio of fact to folderol in their attention to current events.

Cable and digital broadcasts—technically not New Media but different from traditional media—likewise permit heaping Orwellian scorn (an attitude) in ways that conventional television networks (Ellul) and radio (Orwell) long trained their producers, reporters, and spokespersons against (professionally acquired [in]aptitudes). "The Daily Show with Jon Stewart" and "The Colbert Report" constituted recent but now outmoded developments. On which network news broadcast would an anchor ask Betsy McCaughey to ground her untruthful hyperbole concerning the Affordable Care Act ["Obamacare"] to show that Ms. McCaughey could not find any passage remotely resembling Ms. McCaughey's claims?[59] Is a news show, even one with extended segments, likely to match Stephen Colbert's demystifications of 21st-century language—as in his very first "THE WØRD" when Mr. Colbert coined "truthiness?"[60]

Obviously, New Media crosscut and fragment audiences such that shared truths become rarer, but we insist that even fractionated media and audiences stand a better chance of rooting out substantial, substantive flimflam than banishing clichés from political writers' prose or other of Orwell's placebos. Orwell defamed politicians for blather and mendacity that masked indefensible acts and motives but prescribed no remedies for élites, politicos, or parties other than pedantry for political writers. Twentieth- and 21st-century writers, critics, and academics might insist that one who wanted to police political language should directly ridicule élites and politicos who mislead rather than depend on political writers to deconstruct public relations and propaganda. Maybe attitude matched to aptitude would be as contagious as he presumed in his final paragraph. However effective one judges fact-checking to have been in recent elections, fact-checkers and reality-based scholars seem to us to have made some headway.[61] A reality-based community amid pseudocracy, fact-checkers often act as if they are vulnerable to charges of bias. Fact-checkers informed by Orwell's semantics [euphemisms, clichés, swindles, and perversions] should feel less vulnerable to criticism.[62]

For Orwellian attitude that leads to debunking aptitude we look to media old and new that demand documentation, an indispensable habit that becomes over time a dynamic aptitude. Decidedly narrow but promising, cyber-commenting is a medium by which participants may expose blather albeit via banter. Electronic comments sections sometimes feature demands for authoritative sources and other verification.[63] Reviews and comments on reviews at amazon.com and similar centers may lower the tone of criticism, but they also propound attitudes that are decidedly un[der]represented in mass and élite reviews and on occasion exhibit aptitudes for discernment.

Conventional broadcast media can assist consumers in practicing skepticism and in rejecting truthiness on—regrettably rare—occasions. The MSNBC gabfest "Morning Joe" in early 2017 banished Trump adviser Kelly-anne Conway from their program when Ms. Conway's "alternative facts" too blatantly deviated from shared reality. While we await similar dismissals of male practitioners of truthy deceptions from the ranks of politicos other than Donald Trump, we draw hope from the notion that some deceit might not be tolerated and some deceivers might be banned from exacerbating pseudocracy. In this instance, then, we hope for but do not expect mass media to develop Orwellian aptitudes.[64]

We should extend Orwell's attitude to those who consume news, but at best we may do so partially. Orwell may have hectored writers because badgering readers and listeners would presume that readers and listeners were much more sensitive or discerning than they seemed to have been [and seem still to be]. Some readers, perhaps most readers, lie safe from turns of phrase that they never read or hear but nonetheless are vulnerable to clichés and catchphrases. Current Events Mavens and prisoners of echo chambers may be insensate to the most common phrases and shibboleths unless those phrases and shibboleths favor their niche or clique or torment an opposing niche or clique. Active ideologues and partisans often devour fibs and fictions so ravenously that phrasing is beside the point. For all of the above, "Politics and the English Language" may be beside any point.

Still, we espy in the New Media referenced above 21st-century consumers capable of parsing and demystifying. Might Orwell's essay, properly updated, profit them? Perhaps the punditocracy, diverted for a moment or two from prosecuting ideological and partisan causes, might yet justify "Politics and the English Language" as a substantial response to the spiral of decline against which Orwell exhorted political writers in 1945. Or perhaps New Media affording technological advances may help direct Orwellian skepticism at the punditocracy.

Small-scale aptitudes such as those paraded above are doubtless a subset of the techniques and means by which modern writers and readers might address some of the devious and deceitful communications of politicos. These aptitudes will not suffice to reverse spiraling pseudocracy any more than Orwell's paltry rules would brake the spiral of decline that he asserted. Nonetheless, attitudes that instill aptitudes seem to us far more effective than any of Orwell's prescriptions.

Section Five—Conclusion

Orwell's large-scale diagnosis in "Politics and the English Language," less than apt for political **writers** in 1945–46, serves as an apt warning for political **readers** in the 21st century. That was and is Irony One. Based on Irony One, we suggest that readers should acquire from "Politics and the English Language" **attitudes** that, practiced and disciplined, may abet **aptitudes** for resistance to and perhaps for reversal of some truthiness and pseudocracy of both politics and the English language in the present century.[65] If readers [and writers] derive from the essay the means by which to resist badinage and blather, then they will revamp the essay and justify instructors in encouraging students to read it closely and thoughtfully. If not, then "Politics and the English Language" will remain a title that educated people are supposed to revere even as the lessons of the essay most useful for present-day politicking and communicating continue to disintegrate into vestiges of pedantry.

As cures, the remedies in this chapter are small bore and small beer. Still, their scope is larger than Orwell's questions and rules restricted to political writers. If our remedies have little more potential to redress shortcomings than his, they certainly have no less. What they do have is greater relevance. For all of his thundering about the concrete and the practical, "Politics and the English Language" is remarkably removed from the lives of 21st-century readers. We hope we have made it less removed.

Still, those who agree that Orwell's large-scale diagnosis suits the present pseudocracy far more than postwar England may achieve more by directing readers to Orwell's attitude and to the aptitudes for skepticism and critical thinking that attitude supports. We find that ironic. Such attitudes and aptitudes will foster habits of discernment. **That** should be the want and the wont of those who recommend or assign the essay.

Notes

1. George Orwell, "Politics and the English Language," *Horizon*, April 1946, 252–265.
2. This phrase occurs amid Paragraph 18 of the essay as enumerated in "A Telescoping Graphic of George Orwell's 'Politics and the English Language,'" accessed https://politicsandtheenglishlanguage.info, a website associated with this book.
3. We adopt the classic formulation in C. Wright Mills, *The Power Elite* (Oxford: Oxford University Press, 1956).
4. Jacques Ellul, *Propaganda* (New York: Knopf, 1968). Originally published as *Propagandes* (Paris: A. Colin, 1962).
5. This is the third sentence in Paragraph 14 of the essay. Please consult "A Telescoping Graphic of George Orwell's 'Politics and the English Language.'"
6. We need not read Orwell's bold start and modest ending as a deliberate bait and switch. Instead we may read Orwell's capacious beginning and crabbed ending as a common prose strategy. Writers often elicit attention by exaggerating the stakes of an essay and then, when they are confident that they have readers' attention, they settle down to concrete specifics.
7. Please note that Orwell was characterizing the arguments of others when he introduced the idea of a general collapse.
8. We want to be fair to Mr. Orwell. Our reading of the second paragraph of "Politics and the English Language" is that Orwell in his first sentence introduces ultimate political and economic causes of linguistic decline mostly to move from such distant, irremediable causes to more immediate, perhaps remediable factors in the decline of politics and language. We two think he does so to overcome any rebuttal that little or nothing can be done about mutually destructive politicking and writing, for such a rebuttal might turn readers and potential converts away. Orwell in his very next sentence turns from ultimate causes to proximate patterns, the habits and usages about which he and other writers might do something. Hence, we two do not claim and do not want to be misunderstood to claim that he pulled some bait and switch by posing a cosmic cataclysm to which he attached puny, pedantic remedies. We two read Orwell to move from passivity and despair concerning ultimate causes about which nothing could be done to activity and optimism about how politico-linguistic decline might be arrested or reversed.
9. We two find it interesting that we must introduce readers to "Politics and the English Language" because Orwell lavished attention on the role of readers for writers in George Orwell, *Why I Write* (New York: Penguin Books, 2005).

10. In his novels, George Orwell, *Animal Farm* (New York: Signet, 1962) and George Orwell, *1984* (New York: Signet, 1950), Orwell dramatized how relatively authoritarian or absolutely totalitarian tyrants abused language to sap the ruled while proclaiming rulers to be about the work and will of the people, so it should not surprise us that in "Politics and the English Language" (1946) Orwell presumed that the powerful in less authoritarian regimes abused language to dominate the credulous powerless.

11. Christopher Hitchens in his introduction to *George Orwell Diaries* claimed that Orwell's World War Two service for the British Broadcasting Corporation led him to see how liberal-democratic Britain shaped history and made names if not persons disappear from the news as suited the interests or desires of the British government or its allies. Christopher Hitchens, "Introduction," in *George Orwell Diaries*, ed. Peter Davison (New York: Liveright Publishing Corporation, 2009; introduction copyright 2012), xiii.

    Please keep in mind that in linking Orwell's conception of political usage to parties, we hew to one of his most memorable phrases: "Political language—and with variations this is true of all political parties, from Conservatives to Anarchists—is designed to make lies sound truthful and murder respectable, and to give an appearance of solidity to pure wind."

12. We acknowledge our snark in mimicking Orwell's five specimens in the essay. We remind our readers that we play off what we regard as his best formulations, whereas Orwell located five woeful specimens and deceitfully called them representative. We alluded to flaws of the "specimens" in Chapter 2; we dissect those "specimens" in Chapter 4.

13. We deem it unkind to note that Orwell's simplicity and directness in this pair of sentences did not save him from stupid remarks.

14. We appropriate phrases from two great social theorists herein. We quote Keynes's famous characterization of politics and ideas to describe **a** relationship and perhaps **the** relationship among purveyors, conveyors, and writers: "Madmen in authority, who hear voices in the air, are distilling their frenzy from some academic scribbler of a few years back." John Maynard Keynes, *The General Theory of Employment, Interest and Money* (Harcourt, Brace & World, 1965), 383. The notion that words may succeed while policies fail—indeed, words may be selected to succeed to obscure policy failures—we took from Murray Edelman, *Political Language: Words That Succeed and Policies That Fail* (Cambridge, MA: Academic Press, 1977).

15. Please contrast Orwell's pedantic semantics with Victor Klemperer's systematic and systemic semantics in *The Language of the Third Reich: LTI—Lingua Tertii Imperii: A Philologist's Notebook* (London: Continuum International Publishing Group, 2006). Please keep in mind, however, that Orwell was dashing off an essay while Klemperer was reflecting rigorously.

16. We do not dwell on what might be Orwell's naïve notion(s) of public opinion and of the political sway of writers because we cannot be sure what he presumed about either.

17. Perhaps Orwell regarded "lies, evasions, folly, hatred, and schizophrenia" to be "vivid" writing. We coauthors regard the quoted language to be hyperbole at best.

18. We realize that television was at most nascent when Orwell wrote the essay. The images to which we refer might be elicited by newspaper copy, radio scripts, and other verbal stimuli.

19. Please note that Orwell invoked at the end of the inset passage the summoning or suppressing of mental pictures as a prominent feature of labeling and design of politicking. This matched his assertion that metaphors exist (solely?) to induce targets to visualize.

20. See Geoffrey Nunberg's, "Simpler Terms; If It's Orwellian, It's Not," *The New York Times*, June 22, 2003, accessed December 2, 2017, www.nytimes.com/2003/06/22/weekinreview/simpler-terms-if-it-s-orwellian-it-s-probably-not.html. Orwell's essay may contradict Nunberg's instructive thesis in that Orwell provides examples of verbal folderol that is exactly the sort of silly euphemizing and sloganeering that Nunberg seems to oppose our calling "Orwellian."

21. We do not imply that Orwell should have been cognizant of Ellul's analyses. Ellul published *Propagandes* in 1962. The English translation *Propaganda: The Formation of Men's Attitudes* appeared in 1968. Orwell died in 1950.

22. We dub consumers in Ellul's work "Current Events Mavens" because Ellul's term, "Current Events Man," might be sexist. (We wanted to write "might be thought sexist" but that would involve a needless passive).

23. By "infotainment" we mean news that values reliable information but delivers it entertainingly to draw ratings or circulation. We believe that Orwell would have excoriated "infotainment" had he lived to see it. Nonetheless, his marked preference for vivid writing over dull, hackneyed writing corresponds to mass media's proclivity for the attention-arresting. Please see "Infotainment," last modified November 27, 2017, https://en.wikipedia.org/wiki/Infotainment. A jeremiad against infotainment vivid enough to please even Eric Arthur Blair may be found in Neil Postman, *Amusing Ourselves to Death: Public Discourse in the Age of Show Business* (New York: Penguin Books, 2005).

24. We stress concreteness because Orwell repeatedly excoriated abstract, ambiguous phrases that supplanted concrete, clear terms in political writing.

25. Regarding normalization, please see W. Lance Bennett, *News: The Politics of Illusion* (New York: Longman 1983). Please compare Stephen Chibnall, *Law-and-Order News: An Analysis of Crime Reporting in the British Press* (London: Routledge Reprint, 2013).

26. Audacious as Frank Luntz was to subtitle *Words That Work: It's Not What You Say, It's What People Hear*, his primer is among the best introductions to mendacity in American marketing. Dr. Luntz shows that the modern media system works by inducing targets to complement catchphrases that are not demonstrably untrue with inferences that are far from proven or probable. Dr. Luntz's claim to be about the agenda that George Orwell set for himself is absurd other than in the limited sense that Luntz "bridges" between Orwell's world of lies and Ellul's world of suffusing truths. Frank I. Luntz, *Words That Work: It's Not What You Say, It's What People Hear* (New York: Hatchette Books, 2007).

27. We do not bother to note every instance in which Orwell violated Orwell's rules for composition. He admitted he had violated his own rules in the promulgation of those rules. However, we draw attention to Orwell's use of "schizophrenia" where "madness" or "insanity" would do and might be equally lurid but less inaccurate (and shorter).

28. "Most people who bother with the matter at all would admit that the English language is in a bad way, but it is generally assumed that we cannot by conscious action do anything about it." The initial clause features an unworthy presumption/subterfuge. The second independent clause uses a passive construction that Orwell ought to edit were he following his own rules.

29. Still less, of course, could Orwell's stylistic fixes remedy the systematic propagandizing that Ellul revealed and analyzed.
30. Our focus in this book is almost exclusively American, yet pseudocracy is far from solely or strictly American. Orwell's United Kingdom is the focus of Peter Oborne's, *The Rise of Political Lying* (London: Simon & Schuster, 2005). F. G. Bailey did not restrict his review to the United States in *The Prevalence of Deceit* (Ithaca, NY: Cornell University Press, 1991).
31. William Butler Yeats, "To a Friend Whose Work Has Come to Nothing," accessed December 2, 2017, www.bartleby.com/147/6.html. We have used "define dishonesty downward" in homage to Daniel Patrick Moynihan's "Defining Deviancy Down," *The American Scholar* 62, no. 1 (1993): 17–23.
32. "Truthiness is what you want the facts to be, as opposed to what the facts are. What feels like the right answer as opposed to what reality will support [sic]." "Truthiness," *Wikiality*, accessed December 2, 2017, wikiality. wikia.com/Truthiness. Stephen Colbert so defined "truthiness" on the inaugural episode of "The Colbert Report" (17 October 2005) and we herein adhere to coiner's intent. Accessed 10 December 2012, www.colbertnation. com/the-colbert-report-videos/24039/october-17-2005/the-word-truthiness. See also Accessed 9 December 2012, www.americandialect.org/Words_of_ the_Year_2005.pdf.
33. Truthy politics and language predominate in modern U.S. politicking, but of course the dominant content of politics consists in mainstream contentions and conventions. These, it could be argued, have always been truthy: reassuring images of and fantasies about reality rather than empirical descriptions.
34. Farhad Manjoo, *True Enough: Learning to Live in a Post-Fact Society* (New York: Wiley, 2008). Of course, before Manjoo created his subtitle, Carl Bybee wrote of a post-factual age. Carl Bybee, "Can Democracy Survive in the Post-Factual Age? A Return to the Lippmann-Dewey Debate about the Politics of News," *Association for Education in Journalism and Mass Communication* 1, no. 1 (1999): 28.
35. When those who espouse truthy certainties are induced or compelled to defend their certainties outside the cozy confines of their factions or their media, incredulity ensues. See, for example, Betsy McCaughey fail to defend her contentions on "The Daily Show with John Stewart," accessed August 1, 2013, www. thedailyshow.com/ watch/thu-august-20-2009/betsy-mccaughey-pt-1.
36. For example, campaigns issue statements that are "literally accurate but inferentially false," in Kathleen Hall Jamieson's fine phrase. See, for example, "Romney China-Made Jeep Comments Fuel Campaign Flashpoint," accessed December 2, 2017, www.bloomberg.com/news/2012-10-30/romney-china-made-jeep-comments-fuel-campaign-flashpoint.html.
37. Dr. John Lott demonstrated how shrewd phrasing served his advantage far more than repeating clichés or violating other of Orwell's rules could have. Please savor how cunningly and carefully Dr. Lott concocted the statement: "With just one single exception, the attack on congresswoman Gabrielle Giffords in Tucson in 2011, every public shooting since at least 1950 in the U.S. in which more than three people have been killed has taken place where citizens are not allowed to carry guns." John Lott, "Two Multiple Victim Public Shootings Have Taken Place Where Guns Were [sic] Concealed Handguns Are Allowed," *John Lott's Website*, accessed January 18, 2013, http://johnrlott.blogspot. com/2013/01/two-multiple-victim-public-shootings.html.

38. We hope that readers note that "spin," "casuistry," and "talking points" often serve as polite terms for lying, misleading, and pettifogging.
39. Please see Ronald N. Jacobs and Eleanor Townsley, *The Space of Opinion: Media Intellectuals and the Public Sphere* (New York: Oxford University Press, 2011); and Eric Alterman, *Sound and Fury: The Making of the Punditocracy* (Ithaca, NY: Cornell University Press, 2000).
40. Please compare at our website Rather-gate and Benghazi.
41. Eric Hoffer made "the true believer" a popular label for political and religious fanatics who surrender their rationality and practicality to demagogues, charismatic hustlers, and totalitarian causes. Eric Hoffer, *The True Believer: Thoughts on the Nature of Mass Movements* (New York: Harper, 1951).
42. Manjoo provides case studies of such true believers and hypothesizes some sociopsychological explanations for factional truths.
43. Characterizations of truth and falsity and of veracity and mendacity vary just as truth-telling and falsehood-spreading vary. When President Harry S Truman proclaimed that he did not give Republicans hell but told the truth about Republicans and Republicans thought it hell—if indeed President Truman said such rather than some flak fabricated it—he may have believed that his accounts were reasonably accurate, but he must have admitted that he spun the record to the advantage of himself and the Democratic Party. Still, as far as we know President Truman's conceits about verity and falsity stopped short of egregious prevarication. Alas, the same could not plausibly be claimed of most of President Truman's successors.
44. Need we add that over time absolute truth(s) and absolute falsehood(s) or lying may shift, thereby stretching continua of verisimilitude to a greater degree?
45. F. G. Bailey defines multiple gradients from truth to its many opposites in Bailey, *The Prevalence of Deceit*, Ch. 1 and xvii.
46. We play here a bit with Moynihan, "Defining Deviancy Down," 17.
47. At the website associated with this book, please see our discussion of Professor Harry Frankfurt's analysis of "bullshit" and "bullshitting." Harry Frankfurt, *On Bullshit* (Princeton, NJ: Princeton University Press, 2005). Among other points, we juxtapose how Dr. Frankfurt discusses sincerity with how Orwell posited that insincerity led to a lack of clarity.
48. We also fear we shall end up with palliatives no better than Orwell's!
49. We take New Media to include content that users may access on their own schedule at any time on the Internet, the World Wide Web, social media, and other digital vehicles. As often is the case in 21st-century socializing and politicking, marketing leads the way: Mark W. Schaefer, *Social Media Explained: Untangling the World's Most Misunderstood Business Trend* (Louisville, KY: Schaefer Marketing Solutions 2014); Jan Zimmerman and Deborah Ng, *Social Media Marketing: All-in-One*, 4th ed. (New York: Wiley, 2017).
50. "Fisking," *Wikipedia*, accessed October 31, 2017, https://en.wikipedia.org/wiki/Robert_Fisk#Fisking. While we realize that many academics find citation to Wikipedia beneath them, we cite that source to establish that fisking is at least somewhat known outside academia.
51. Forgotten it already? That is just our point! "I am not, indeed, sure whether it is not true to say that the Milton who once seemed not unlike a seventeenth-century Shelley had not become, out of an experience ever more bitter in each year, more alien [sic] to the founder of that Jesuit sect which nothing could induce him to tolerate."

52. "Above all, we cannot play ducks and drakes with a native battery of idioms which prescribes egregious collocations of vocables as the Basic [sic] *put up with* for *tolerate*, or *put at a loss* for *bewilder*."
53. Joan Walsh, "The Stunning Dishonesty of Charles Murray," accessed August 3, 2017, www.salon.com/2014/03/18/paul_krugman_demolishes_charles_mur rays_stunning_racist_dishonesty/.
54. Regarding the maxim that a witness false in one detail may be distrusted in other or all details, please see accessed April 13, 2017, https://definitions. uslegal.com/f/falsus-in-uno-falsus-in-omnibus/. Examples of small-scale, simple assessments of the reliability of commentators and editorialists that might complement point-by-point fisking are available at the website associated with this book.
55. Please see examples at accessed February 18, 2018, www.techlicious.com/ guide/the-best-news-aggregation-sites/.
56. For examples please see accessed February 18, 2018, www.politifact.com/ punditfact/ and www.slate.com/articles/news_and_politics/politics/2013/12/ pundit_audit_2013_what_dave_weigel_got_right_and_wrong_in_political_ predictions.html.
57. Please see also Dr. Andrew Sullivan's, "The Dick Morris Award," *The Dish*, accessed December 2, 2017, https://dish.andrewsullivan.com/awards/.
58. Among sites of demystification or outright trashing on the World Wide Web are "Instapundit," accessed December 2, 2017, https//pjmedia.com/instapundit/; "Media Matters for America," accessed December 2, 2017, https://mediamatters. org/; "Fairness and Accuracy in Reporting," accessed December 2, 2017, https:// fair.org/; and "Accuracy in Media," accessed December 2, 2017, www.aim.org.
59. Please see the unmasking of Betsy McCaughey on "The Daily Show," accessed December 2, 2017, www.cc.com/video-clips/b52wbd/the-daily-show-with-jon-stewart-betsy-mccaughey-pt-1 and www.cc.com/video-clips/bv57fl/the-daily-show-with-jon-stewart-exclusive-betsy-mccaughey-extended-interview-pt-2. Ms. McCaughey elicited a "Pants on Fire" from Politifact regarding her claims.
60. Accessed December 2, 2017, www.cc.com/video-clips/63ite2/the-colbert-report-the-word-truthiness.
61. Lest we overload our readers, we do not here rehearse Andrew Chadwick, *The Hybrid Media System: Politics and Power* (New York: Oxford University Press, 2013), which reveals ways in which media new and old overlap and mutually reinforce.
62. Please examine Brooks Jackson and Kathleen Hall Jamieson, *unSpun* (New York: Random House Tradebooks, 2007).
63. Please recall that Orwell's fifth specimen was a letter to an editor, the 1940's technology that comments sections have superseded if not improved.
64. We two may be unduly pessimistic. While social media such as Facebook represent enormous expenditures of time for little profit in aptitudes amid ample attitudes, many postings edify readers and increase their capacities to prefer the verifiable to the welcome.
65. Our attentive readers will espy in this sentence a rhetorical move similar to Orwell's ending of his essay: individual adjustments that might add up to resistance to systemic trends. Our readers must decide whether we two have broadened Orwell's semantic tweaks and forensic taunts into more active tactics for reading and responding.

Bibliography

Alterman, Eric. *Sound and Fury: The Making of the Punditocracy*. Ithaca, NY: Cornell University Press, 2000.

Bailey, F. G. *The Prevalence of Deceit*. Ithaca, NY: Cornell University Press, 1991.

Bennett, W. Lance. *News: The Politics of Illusion*. New York: Longman, 1983.

Bybee, Carl. "Can Democracy Survive in the Post-Factual Age? A Return to the Lippmann-Dewey Debate about the Politics of News." *Association for Education in Journalism and Mass Communication* 1, no. 1 (1999): 28.

Chadwick, Andrew. *The Hybrid Media System: Politics and Power*. New York: Oxford University Press, 2013.

Chibnall, Stephen. *Law-and-Order News: An Analysis of Crime Reporting in the British Press*. London: Routledge Reprint, 2013.

Edelman, Murray. *Political Language: Words That Succeed and Policies That Fail*. Cambridge, MA: Academic Press, 1977.

Ellul, Jacques. *Propaganda*. New York: Knopf, 1968.

Ellul, Jacques. *Propagandes*. Paris: A. Colin, 1962.

Hitchens, Christopher. "Introduction." In *George Orwell Diaries*, edited by Peter Davison, ix–xvii. New York: Liveright Publishing Corporation, 2009; introduction copyright 2012.

Hoffer, Eric. *The True Believer: Thoughts on the Nature of Mass Movements*. New York: Harper, 1951.

Jackson, Brooks, and Kathleen Hall Jamieson. *unSpun*. New York: Random House Tradebooks, 2007.

Jacobs, Ronald N., and Eleanor Townsley. *The Space of Opinion: Media Intellectuals and the Public Sphere*. New York: Oxford University Press, 2011.

Keynes, John Maynard. *The General Theory of Employment, Interest and Money*. Harcourt, Brace & World, 1965.

Klemperer, Victor. *The Language of the Third Reich: LTI—Lingua Tertii Imperii: A Philologist's Notebook*. London: Continuum International Publishing Group, 2006.

Lott, John. "Two Multiple Victim Public Shootings Have Taken Place Where Guns Were [sic] Concealed Handguns Are Allowed." *John Lott's Website*. Accessed January 18, 2013. http://johnrlott.blogspot.com/2013/01/two-multiple-victim-public-shootings.html.

Luntz, Frank I. *Words That Work: It's Not What You Say It's What People Hear*. New York: Hatchette Books, 2007.

Manjoo, Farhad. *True Enough: Learning to Live in a Post-Fact Society*. New York: Wiley, 2008.

Moynihan, Daniel Patrick. "Defining Deviancy Down." *The American Scholar* 62, no. 1 (1993): 17–23.

Nunberg, Geoffrey. "Simpler Terms; If It's Orwellian, It's Not." *The New York Times*, June 22, 2003. Accessed December 2, 2017. www.nytimes.com/2003/06/22/weekinreview/simpler-terms-if-it-s-orwellian-it-s-probably-not.html.

Osborne, Peter. *The Rise of Political Lying*. London: Simon and Schuster, 2005.

Orwell, George. *1984*. New York: Signet, 1950.

Orwell, George. *Animal Farm*. New York: Signet, 1962.

Orwell, George. "Politics and the English Language." *Horizon*, April 1946, 252–265.

Orwell, George. *Why I Write*. New York: Penguin Books, 2005.

Postman, Neil. *Amusing Ourselves to Death: Public Discourse in the Age of Show Business*. New York: Penguin Books, 2005.

Schaefer, Mark W. *Social Media Explained: Untangling the World's Most Misunderstood Business Trend*. Louisville, KY: Schaefer Marketing Solutions, 2014.

Walsh, Joan. "The Stunning Dishonesty of Charles Murray." Accessed August 3, 2017. www.salon.com/2014/03/18/paul_krugman_demolishes_charles_murrays_stunning_racist_dishonesty/.

Wikiality. "Truthiness." Accessed December 2, 2017. http://wikiality.wikia.com/wiki/Truthiness.

Wikipedia. "Fisking." Accessed October 31, 2017. https://en.wikipedia.org/wiki/Robert_Fisk#Fisking.

Wikipedia. "Infotainment." Accessed November 27, 2017. https://en.wikipedia.org/wiki/Infotainment.

Yeats, William Butler. "To a Friend Whose Work Has Come to Nothing." Accessed December 2, 2017. www.bartleby.com/147/6.html.

Zimmerman, Jan, and Deborah Ng. *Social Media Marketing: All-in-One*. 4th ed. New York: Wiley, 2017.

4 Orwell's *Corpora Delectorum*

How Orwell's Memorable Offenses Have Obscured Orwell's Forgotten Thesis

We chide Orwell's chafing spirit by titling this chapter with a Latin phrase that means "bodies of crimes"[1] to herald our examination of Orwell's attacks on felonious writing. In this chapter we recount Orwell's offenses against writers and writing in "Politics and the English Language" to elaborate the second irony that we unveiled in Chapter 1: Orwell's provocative gripes and gibes may provide us highbrow infotainment, but that entertainment in the guise of intellectual argument has long obscured what Orwell claimed the largest-scale point of his essay to be. To back up that second irony, we accuse him of diversionary prose. Labeling him an Overreaching Prosecutor, then an Overbearing Pedant, and then an Overlooking Parodist, we argue that he entertains greatly but enlightens less in doing so. In our view, Orwell's intellectual infotainment almost guaranteed that his trenchant prosecution, pedantry, and parody would be recalled more often and more fondly than would the alarum from which he began his essay.

Section One—Orwell as Overreaching Prosecutor

Orwell's five exhibits pilloried five authors for language-crimes he did not prove. Far more than "mental vices" or "bad habits" that Orwell proclaimed widespread, his five "specimens" illustrate malicious prosecution of two professors by name and of three unnamed defendants. In his five indictments, he played the overzealous, overweening accuser by whom only a jury of credulous, inattentive, under-informed readers—such as the coauthors for so long—could be persuaded.

Two or three considerations quash Orwell's first indictment. The first defendant, Professor Laski, exemplified academic folly—conjuring needless difficulty and seeming originality from a simple, ordinary observation—more than any vices political or mental. Apparently Laski meant to claim that comparing politically alert poet Milton to politically alert, and radical, poet Shelley might make sense and certainly isn't outlandish. He garbled the message with the silly quadruple negative (with a twist and in the pike position!), and he may have done so because he was being too cautious, like many academics who have adapted to the pedantic, hypercritical niche they inhabit. If we are right about this indictment, it follows that, far from being indifferent to what he was writing or meaning (as Orwell resounded), Professor Laski more likely was fussing over what he might defend as a presumption and got lost in his own (defensive) prose. One miscreant sentence, however, evinces no mental vice nor any bad habit. Indeed, one errant sentence manifests no habit at all!

Prosecutor Orwell then hales into language court a second professor, Lancelot Hogben of "ducks and drakes" fame. His crime was to have produced writing that might spread by imitation and indicate certain mental vices that were imperiling the republic and the discourse.

We may almost effortlessly reject this charge, too, for the quotation from Hogben does not represent malignant political prose or representative mental defects or delicts. Still one or two features of this case, as Sherlock Holmes would say, interest an attentive observer. Before we get to them, we will simply note that Hogben was another academic writing about a subject even more arcane than Laski's business about Milton and Shelley: a language that zoologist and statistician Dr. Hogben had invented. If Orwell were truly seeking "representative" examples of writing made bad by politics and politics made bad by writing, then he probably should not have begun looking in Hogben's invention of an artificial language. We grant him that he has located a sentence likely to make jurors gasp and guffaw, but we insist that on that ground Hogben's fusty, obscure writing is not representative of any other prose, does not exemplify any widespread mental vice, and is unlikely to have exerted any political influence or propagandistic effect by 1945 or thereafter. Prosecutor Orwell has no case against Professor Hogben.

Having pilloried two professors by name, Orwell in his third "specimen" turns to an anonymous reviewer.

We admit that, in his third try, at least Orwell went to a journal called *Politics* to find some language allegedly infested by or with politics. Well played. The trouble is, he selected a passage from an essay on psychology that apparently includes some fuzzy thinking from the pop-psychology of the times. We are still waiting for an example of writing harshly affected by or affecting politics rather than annoying academic habits and are already tiring of discourse that exhibits carelessness about relatively arcane subjects. Having claimed in his opening statement to his readers that widespread habits of poor communication were debilitating politics and language, Prosecutor Orwell for a third time regales his readers with academic prose hardly representative of content with which most readers would bother, with abstruse expression hardly widespread enough to influence most readers if they did persist in reading the passages, and with outlandish pursuits that seem not to bear on, let alone to endanger, politics or the English language.

Nonetheless, reader-juror, let us celebrate. Just when we all were getting impatient with his reckless prosecution, Orwell on his fourth try adduces an example of writing about politics—from a Communist pamphlet.

Of course this fourth example is a bit too easy because it **is** from a Communist pamphlet, and such pamphlets tend to bad writing for insiders who like their writing bad in a very particular way: trafficking in talking points and shibboleths.[2] Such prose is supposed to sate the initiated, so it is successful if you are a Communist having a pint and glancing at a pamphlet some bloke just handed you. For that very reason, however, it is not a good example of everyday journalistic writing much affected by or much affecting politics. If the first three examples are too far from Orwell's major point, then looking in a Communist pamphlet for bad political writing is almost self-fulfilling. Not only is that uncomfortably close to Orwell's planting evidence in his investigation, but it also pushes him further away from a fair representation of the habits and mind-set of political writing that he claimed he would be presenting.

To be fair to Orwell, however, we agree that the fault in the passage **is** primarily with political rhetoric aimed at what the 21st century might call "the base," the true believers. The fault lies not with Communism per se, we should add. For we might adjourn briefly to Twitter or to partisan online sites, where we might find true believers of many political ideologies hurling ugly monikers at one another. We agree that partisan writing predictably goes over the top and repeats clichés as it calls names and otherwise disrespects the opposition. We cannot agree that the example supports Orwell's claim that his era is an especially bad one for political writing. If we read political pamphlets from the 19th century, or political graffiti from the imperial Rome, wouldn't we find examples as excessive and amusing and, well, "political?" If Orwell has located political writing that is political, at least his fourth "specimen" pertains to "Politics and the English Language."

For the purposes of our book and of Orwell's major claim, we are more interested in how people can avoid falling prey to predictably disrespectful language from partisans with whom they are likely to agree. It is easy to spot "foul incendiarism" in prose from one's political opponents, but to preserve clear thinking, it is more important to spot and to openly acknowledge foul incendiarism wherever one finds it, even in prose from people with whose political positions one agrees. Still, Orwell **has** caught a pamphleteer behaving like a pamphleteer, and pamphleteers often manifest mental vices and bad habits that bear on politics.

If Orwell's fourth defendant comes closest to manifesting poor prose habits and mental vices, his fifth target, taken from a letter to a newspaper about the BBC, may lie the furthest from Orwell's explicit object.

We regard Orwell's fifth target as his bummest rap because we read the letter-writer to be indulging herself or himself, having a good time with politics and with language, and suffering from no linguistic, political, or other ills that we can diagnose. Citizen John Doe wants the BBC (British Broadcasting Corporation) to let in working-class speech, which the writer thinks is more virile. Given what the BBC sounded like back then, and sounds like now, that is an intentionally amusing idea, right out of Monty Python. But then the writer expresses the view in writing that sounds awfully (*double entendre* intended) BBC-ish. That is, Orwell's letter-writer may be about entertaining himself. Not everyone will get the joke, we concede, but at the same time it is difficult if not impossible for us to see the letter as serious prose negatively affected by or adversely affecting language, politics, or anything else. It's a letter making fun of BBC-speak in a way that is at least playful and probably also self-mocking, especially upon a second reading. It is not an example of language corrupted by propaganda or politics, and it does seem to show the writer was aware of the amusing excesses in the prose. Maybe the letter-writer's point was serious: Let's hear some working-class syllables on the BBC! But the mode of his message is all in good fun, like it (the mode) or not. Orwell missed the joke, possibly because the joke wasn't good enough, or because he was in no humorous mood, or both. At any rate, the example does not exemplify a "mental vice" of the sort he has in mind in his prosecutor's opening statement.

Irony Two applies with full force to this section of "Politics and the English Language," then: The overwhelming evidence Orwell pretended to present underwhelms, at best. That Orwell is not in on the joke in "specimen five," was not down with Communist patter in "specimen four," was unimpressed by academese in "specimen three," was aghast at the artificial language proffered by a zoologist and statistician in "specimen two," and found a "fairly representative" quadruple or quintuple negative in "specimen one" should not push any reader of Orwell's essay past reasonable doubts. Based on Prosecutor Orwell's exhibits, we ask our readers to issue a directed verdict in favor of all five accused.

So what do the five examples represent if they do not represent politically corrupted or corrupting language? Probably they represent writing that annoyed Orwell. At most, then, Prosecutor Orwell has one or more of the five defendants on a petty misdemeanor: sloppiness in the nth degree or failure to proofread or some such. We coauthors spot no felonious writing in any of the passages that Prosecutor Orwell brandished.

We established in Chapter 2 that Orwell's "specimens" related to his thesis little or not at all. That is one way in which his examples did not suffice. We have now shown a second insufficiency in Prosecutor Orwell's exhibits: His five examples do not quite exemplify poor prose!

Was Orwell in such a rush during that busy year he had no time to find passages from prose significantly damaged by political thinking? Possibly. Had Prosecutor Orwell thought through well enough what he meant by "mental vices?" Perhaps not. Are the five examples good evidence of mental vices or representative of habits of writing? No.

Having neither *corpus delecti* nor *corpora delectora*—that is, no victims of the felony to whom Orwell can persuasively point jurors—Procurator[3] Orwell perpetrated a show trial. We do not want to believe that of Orwell, but we have yet to suppose an alternative explanation.

Section Two—Orwell as Overbearing Pedant

Barely has Orwell called the specimens' labor-saving devices "tricks" when he assails "dying metaphors," "operators or verbal false limbs," "pretentious diction," and "meaningless words" in what he then calls a "catalogue of swindles and perversions." We now track Orwell's transforming labor-saving tricks into swindles and perversions to show that Orwell is far more persuasive regarding writers' labor-saving, perhaps even lazy, habits than he is in establishing those four habits and alleged mental vices as swindles or perversions that somehow threaten England or English. He expressed his four headings vividly, a pepping-up of prose that George Orwell endorsed repeatedly. As a result, we two find his headings far more memorable than the more sensible, more insidious particulars that Orwell rendered no less vividly but far more aptly. Too bad those four sorts of "swindles and perversions" are nothing of the sort; still worse that those four sorts may crowd out the excellent "swindles and perversions" with which Orwell regaled his readers.

If by "dying metaphors" (the first item in his catalogue) Orwell meant metaphors or other figures overly familiar, then of course we may agree with him. If writers deploy metaphors or similes, especially in professional writing like opinion pieces, feature writing, trade books, memoir, and literature, they should generate fresh, clear, efficient metaphors and similes, we suppose.[4] However, Orwell's five specimens offer few "dying metaphors" that we can detect. "Ducks and drakes," from Professor Hogben's prose, may be the best example of what Orwell means, and he offers no evidence or argument to establish that "ducks and drakes" was a dying, as opposed to dead, metaphor.[5] As noted, Laski's problem isn't with metaphors, and the same goes for the psychology piece, which is almost free of metaphorical writing. The Communist's pamphlet repeats predictable terms such as "fascist" and "bourgeoisie," but we are not convinced to count these shibboleths as dying-metaphor trickery rather than the boilerplate of orthodoxy that Orwell in his essay described. In the letter, "British lion" probably counts as a dying metaphor, but otherwise the writer seems to be having fun with relatively fresh metaphors and similes, comparing BBC-speak to that of Shakespeare's Bottom (so to speak), and suggesting it is "as gentle as any sucking dove." Not bad at all. We also get the excessively fresh and deliberately florid "school-ma'amish arch braying of blameless bashful mewing maidens!" It is over-written, on purpose, but also entertaining, also on purpose we think. And right before that, we learn that the letter writer agrees with Orwell insofar as he or she thinks BBC-speak is "priggish, inflated, [and] inhibited"—just like Laski's sentence.

As to "operators and verbal false limbs" (the second item in his catalogue), we must confess that we have long found the phrase annoying because we don't know what Orwell took an "operator" to be in this context and because we think that while "verbal false limbs" may be a fresh metaphor, it isn't an especially apt one.[6] We concede that wordiness may spring from trying too hard—which of course is nearly the opposite of the sloth of which he accuses "political writers," but never mind—or from working in a genre with which one is familiar, but does that make a labor-saving, perhaps inadvertent trick devious, vicious, or perverse? Isn't such "taking the long way around the barn" a relatively minor flaw that a political writer might correct in revision? "Make itself felt" may be a bit vague, but does "take effect" sink to the level of deception? "Exhibit a tendency to" is vague and circuitous and springs from an academic, Laski-esque state of mind. "Serve the purpose of" seems clear enough, and although it is dispensable during revision, does it really sound all that pretentious? Is it a trick?

Really the advice we all need to give ourselves as writers, "take more care as you revise," will, when followed, address such wordiness, but otherwise with such problems in constructing prose, one needn't be alert to "mental vices." Wordiness seems to us two to be neither vicious nor immoral, but then, given what you are reading, you could easily guess why we two had better take that stance to escape arrest. It seems to us, in summary, that "operators and verbal false limbs" is Orwell's pedantic recycling of the idea that proofreading and revision are good habits.[7]

We do agree, however, that "pretentious diction" is a bad habit from which many or most academics and other professional pontificators suffer. Orwell is right to excoriate pretentious wording as too often the tool of swindlers and political writers, if not perverts. That said, a discerning writer or savvy reader may not automatically agree that the words Orwell provides as examples are in fact "pretentious." Consider "phenomenon, element, individual (as noun), objective, categorical, effective, virtual, basic, primary, promote, constitute, exhibit, exploit, utilize, eliminate, [and] liquidate" from Orwell's list. A practiced, careful writer or a well-read person can probably think of many instances in which each one of these words would be appropriate or harmless, for much depends on the context and the audience and even on the particular sentence or paragraph that's being constructed. He seems to us to have wanted his readers to agree that "phenomenon," "basic," and "exploit" are always and everywhere "pretentious," but they simply aren't nowadays and, we suspect, weren't in 1945, and in any case each is a matter of writers' judgment, rhetorical savvy, and discernment.

And, looping back once more to Orwell's major claim—"politics corrupts language, which in turn corrupts politics"—isn't the way politicians pretend to sound like "just folks" much more insidious than their trying to sound like they're experts? If Orwell would have fended off swindlers and perverts, he might have done better to worry about pretense itself than about pretentious words. The great tricksters of our age, politicians like President Reagan and President Clinton, struck us as far more menacing when they practiced their down-home, familiar lingo to soothe the masses than when, or if, they strained to sound important. Politicians and pundits are more easily ignored or mocked, we think, when they try to sound smart and informed but come off as pretentious. They're usually doing us a favor by making that mistake. Folksy oversimplifications often present more problems than pretentious constructions, it seems to us.

In like manner deceptive clarity may threaten politics and discourse in ways that Orwell's essay does not pursue but those who teach composition often have. One idea is that the clear prose or public discourse that appeals to many people may sometimes disguise an omission of crucial information.[8] In the case of Reagan's "trickle-down economics," later revived by Mitt Romney's appeal to cut taxes on the "job creators" (rich people), one major omission was the fact that modern industrial economies are driven by the consumer-spending of people who aren't rich, so that government-spending, based on taxes, on job-creation (for examples, money for building highways and bridges) might actually be more effective than waiting for trickling that never or seldom happens or, if it does happen, **only** trickles—by definition. Whether one agrees with the economic analysis is beside our point, however; our point is that slogans such as "trickle-down economics" or "supply-side economics" stifle debate or stultify citizens. Scholars including Crowley, Kintz, and Kreuter suggest that prose-clarity, then, can be an ideological or political gambit whereby cultural pressure to write and speak simply distracts attention from or hides issues that, if discussed properly, would require complex discourse and would make ideological rifts plain and require substantial data as well as the experience and patience to analyze such data.

Jacques Ellul's analysis of propaganda implicitly reinforces the point these composition-scholars adduce, for by using simple language like that used in advertising, propagandists can reliably appeal to the masses in a way that makes individuals believe the communication is targeted (only?) at them, in a familiar, folksy, clear way. That, of course, is a very dangerous pretense.

Having just shown how Orwell's punctilious pedantry misdirected him into going after words when the greater perils lay in the falsehoods the pretentious language was supposed to camouflage, we now note with similar rue that Orwell plunges from pedantic to frantic in misstating his critique of meaningless words, the fourth and final item in his catalogue. We coauthors, two professors, hence two pedants, find "meaningless words" an example of Orwell's pretentious diction, for in that part of his essay he produces exactly no words that are meaningless.

Orwell uses "meaningless" in a peculiar manner. Words are meaningless in his sense when they neither "point to any discoverable object" nor are expected to do so. He illustrates his usage with regard to words that critics wield to appraise art or literature, and then denounces terms that point to no discoverable object and are not expected to do so in politics or governance. "The word *Fascism* has now no meaning except in so far as it signifies 'something not desirable.' " We doubt that "Fascism," especially when capitalized, lacked any meaning beyond bad in 1945. Orwell overstated his point, perhaps unintentionally. He then exacerbated his overstatement in his next sentence: "The words *democracy, socialism, freedom, patriotic, realistic, justice* have each of them several different meanings which cannot be reconciled with one another."

We do not want to out-pedant Orwell, so we do not ask "Which is it, sir? Are the words without meaning or do they have too many irreconcilable meanings?" Instead, we note that he is making the helpful point that terms by which writers convey approval or disapproval often have multiple denotations and many connotations. We insist, we hope non-pedantically, that the multiplicity of meanings contradicts any claim that Orwell's examples are meaningless. Thus, while we admire the point that political writers deliberately deceive their readers by encouraging or allowing readers to attach this denotation or that connotation to a word without the writer's committing herself or himself to a definition, we insist that Orwell is presuming multiple meanings rather than absence of meaning, ambiguities or equivocation rather than vagueness. He intones, "Other words used in variable meanings, in most cases more or less dishonestly, are: *class, totalitarian, science, progressive, reactionary, bourgeois, equality.*" The variable meanings of those terms make them far from meaningless, however.

As regarding "pretentious diction" so regarding "meaningless words:" Orwell did not write what he meant (or what he ought to have meant). He meant to indict equivocation or double talk. Political writers, Orwell meant to argue, through routine, expediency, and sloth turn to terms that might be literally or lexically defensible—the cunning writer's escape route!—but that may conceal as much as reveal. Facile reliance on jargon and clichés enables political writers to **be** elusive and evasive while **seeming** incisive or insightful, rendering readers certain when they should be wary and persuaded when they should find writing unclear.

Orwell writes that his four "tricks" political writers use to dodge the work of constructing prose make up some "catalogue of swindles and perversions," but that retrospective characterization, we think it plain, is unwarranted for the four tricks, albeit merited for particular examples. Indeed, Orwell seems to us to move from pedantry to legalistic or moralistic excess, especially when we recall that he purports to have derived the tricks and dodges from five specimens. Professor Laski's sentence, more to be pitied than scorned, may be an academic dodge (as we have admitted above), but Professor Laski thereby tricked no reader astute enough to peruse (and to persevere through) an "Essay on Freedom of Expression." Professor Hogben's sentence perhaps betokens haste or sloppiness but seems scarcely likely to swindle anyone or pervert anything; it's just a little hard to follow. The sentence from the Communist pamphlet is too laughably inept to illustrate a mental vice, to trick or to swindle or to pervert anybody or anything. The passage about a free personality is sloppy and casual in the way of pop-psychology, but we find in it nothing vicious, tricky, dodgy, deceptive, or perverted. And we think the letter to the *Times* addresses a serious question about the diction of mass media in a playful way, but even if you are as annoyed with the letter as Orwell was, you may question whether there is, in fact, evidence of trickery or evasion, of swindling or perversion.

Before we conclude that, just as Orwell's prosecution lacked bodies resulting from crimes, Orwell's pedantry lacked bodies of vices, of swindles, of perversions, or of other serious targets, however, let us praise Orwell's deft, telling examples. Please reread the last two quotations from Orwell. Those examples, which we argued did not establish meaninglessness, do seem to us two to include swindles and perversions. If a writer or speaker deploys "fascist" or "fascism" to scorn a person or position with which the writer or speaker disagrees, the writer or speaker may induce members of an audience to pervert the meaning of the term and thereby to swindle themselves into a frenzy neither merited nor productive (except, perhaps, for the speaker or writer). Invocations of "democracy" or "socialism" or "freedom" or "justice" may likewise swindle the unsuspecting and pervert the conversation. To be certain, such symbols or shibboleths tempt communicators to conscious dishonesty. Those who trade in talking points may not even intend to deceive yet may swindle or pervert themselves. In sum, Orwell has produced swindles and perversions in his examples even though he has not established that his list of four tricks descends to the level of swindles or diversions.

Section Three—Orwell as Overlooking Parodist

We turn now from our time to consider clarity, simplicity, obscurity, dying metaphors, pretentious diction, and operators or verbal false limbs to our time to make a big deal of Orwell's wee parody of Ecclesiastes. In that parody Orwell overlooks at least two matters. He not only justifies his parodic flourish by a sequence that he then fails to articulate but also overlooks words that might make passage or parody accurate or true. Indeed, his parody makes the biblical translation less accurate and less true than the King James version. His much-lauded parody, then, displays anew our second, intermediate-level irony: Orwell's showy caricature amuses readers but diverts readers even more from the overall claim that the parody, somehow, is supposed to serve.

Orwell justifies his parody in a transitional remark:

> Now that I have made this catalogue of swindles and perversions, let me give another example of the kind of writing that they lead to. This time it must of its nature be an imaginary one. I am going to translate a passage of good English into modern English of the worst sort. Here is a well-known verse from *Ecclesiastes*:

We two read Orwell to claim that his parody exemplifies consequences of the swindles and perversions, yet he does not complete his point by demonstrating links either to the pedantic catalogue that immediately precedes the parody or to the major claim he set himself in his first two paragraphs. We maintain that he never articulates which swindles or perversions bear on or relate to whatever "kind" of writing he has in mind. We invite our readers to detect in the parody even one feature to which "dying metaphors," "operators or verbal false limbs," "pretentious diction," and "meaningless words" led. We inset Orwell's parody:

> I returned and saw under the sun, that the race is not to the swift, nor the battle to the strong, neither yet bread to the wise, nor yet riches to men of understanding, nor yet favour to men of skill; but time and chance happeneth to them all.

Here it is in modern English:

> Objective considerations of contemporary phenomena compel the conclusion that success or failure in competitive activities exhibits no

tendency to be commensurate with innate capacity, but that a considerable element of the unpredictable must invariably be taken into account.

Do we coauthors overlook some dying metaphors or operators or verbal false limbs or pretentious diction in the parody? Which words of the parody does Orwell take or mean to be meaningless? Can our readers tell us which items in Orwell's catalogue of swindles and perversions led to what features of the caricature?

Even if readers could find connections between Orwell's swindles and perversions and the "kind of writing"—Isn't your own writing a bit too abstract and vague in this transition, George?—to which swindles and perversions lead, Orwell's parody reproduces an untruth to which poetic, figurative, and vivid expressions are liable to a greater degree than prosaic, literal, and dull bureaucratese is. In an essay about muddled writing, Orwell muddles matters the same way in which the King James Bible does. Please reread the original and the parody above. A problem with the biblical verse was highlighted in a waggery perhaps 100 years old: "The race may not be to swift nor the battle to the strong, but that is the way to bet."[9] Orwell selected a poetic original that is missing adverbs or other qualifiers. Races **usually** go to the swift, for that is a common definition of swiftness. Battles **often** do go to the strong. We grant the Bible poetic license and admit that plenty of readers will get the passage's point, but we insist that as written the sentence is not quite true.[10] In other words, in constructing his parody, Orwell faithfully reproduces the absence of qualifiers or other devices by which to make the sentence make more sense. Orwell makes matters worse. Please check us on this issue by reading the parody again.

Even the poetic King James Bible does not go so far as "no tendency" or "invariably" push this sentence. Mr. Orwell overlooks clarity and sense in constructing his parody. We coauthors take that to be a common hazard of parody as well as of pedantry.

Orwell's parody is at least as funny as the letter to the *Times* (specimen five). The parody amuses because it captures a humorless urge all of us may sometimes indulge when we are trying to turn observation into concept or, in this instance, caution. Orwell successfully transmogrifies the poetry of Ecclesiastes into the risible prose of much technical or social scientific writing and of many books about business or economics. That far, that good.

Any further, however, quite bad. As Orwell ridicules business-speak or academese[11] in a striking manner impertinent to his overall claim, his comically dull rendering of a classic verse from a widely admired text is such a memorable distraction that most readers probably miss that Orwell asserts what he cannot come close to proving. A discerning reader will ask why, if stuffy, over-serious, specialized writing is corroding English and politics alike, Orwell must construct a hypothetical rather than cite some actual examples. Most readers, however, will be and have been enthralled by Orwell's infotainment. Many will sit back and enjoy his show.

Orwell's own analysis of his parody explicitly exacerbates his misdirection. Concentrated mainly on vivid, concrete writing, Orwell wrote, "The whole tendency of modern prose is away from concreteness." The whole tendency of this sentence seems to be to assert an impossibly broad generalization. Moreover, we think that, as on-target as the parody and Orwell's analysis of it may seem, Orwell misses or misuses differences between poetry and prose or, as we hateful academics might put the matter, masks the issue of genre. Poetry often depends upon writing rhythmically and usually involves evoking imagery in ways that prose genres necessarily don't or don't necessarily. One could imagine another parody in which the prose discusses a political issue in the poetic style of Whitman or Poe, and that parody, too, might get a laugh from the discord between genres, but it, too, would demonstrate no "whole tendency" of modern prose.

To wax even more broadly and academically, we remind our readers that many kinds of verbal expression and analyses are conceptual and abstract by their nature. Political writing routinely invokes economics, philosophy, theology, social studies, and science, writing that seasoned readers expect to be less vivid than the sentence from Ecclesiastes. We enjoy vivid, rhythmic writing as much as Orwell, but we tend to shy away from writing too concrete or too vivid because the authors of such writings tend to discard complexity and to stunt analysis and argument. We might go too far if we suggest that Orwell—like Plato in dialogues starring the recurring character Socrates—pits his parodic version of hypothetical academic writing against a poetic verse from an enduring King James translation of the Bible. (Gee, Ecclesiastes won? A shocker!) So let us be far less vivid and far more concrete: Orwell's parody doesn't represent well any tendency whole or partial, but it does overlook audience, rhetoric, and genre. Other than that, we coauthors liked the spectacle as well.

The more charming Orwell's parody is, the more it distracts from Orwell's larger point. Indeed, most of Orwell's readers likely miss that the concoction is easy to follow and faithfully rehearses the moral of the passage from Ecclesiastes even if it wrecks the vivid, rhythmic writing. We wonder if the very showiness of the parody—its literary infotainment value—makes it memorable and thereby obscures the now-distant thesis that the parody might have been supposed to serve.

In the matter of Orwell's parody, then, Orwell plants the *corpus delecti*—the body or the most basic fact of an offense—to frame unnamed, unknown, indeed unreal writers. He perpetrates hypothetical language-crime to supplant the actual evidence he would need to substantiate "the whole tendency of modern prose." That's a neat trick. That is a perversion of argument. That's infotainment!

Section Four—Orwell's Not Un-Prosecutorial, Not Un-Pedantic, Not Un-Parodic Misdirection and Irony Two

We have shown that essayist George Orwell—a.k.a. Eric Arthur Blair, a.k.a. The Overreaching Prosecutor, a.k.a. The Overbearing Pedant, a.k.a. The Overlooking Parodist—got in the way of his explicit thesis at least as much as he tried his case, picked his nits, and skewered his targets. That, the reader may recall, is our second, intermediate-level irony. Orwell seized his readers' attention and for that reason dominated his readers' recollections to such an extent that his gripes, gibes, and grousing crowd out the thesis he had purported to be serving. We do not see how or where he connected to the case that he stated he would be making: either his memorable dissection of his five specimens or his noteworthy and thus noted catalogue of so-called swindles and so-called perversions or his striking mockery of Ecclesiastes. Beyond that foible common to great writers as well as to lesser writers such as the coauthors of this monograph, we two read these sections of "Politics and the English Language" to lie at cross-purposes with the alleged aim of the whole. Orwell may have hoped that his commentary on his five specimens, the four items in his catalogue, and his parody might have clarified his meaning in his first and second paragraphs;[12] we think he dashed his express hope because his vivid, arresting prose diverted his readers from the meaning he claimed to be on about.

We two hope we are not gratuitous to illustrate Orwell's misdirecting (if not misinforming) his readers in a memorable manner (Irony Two) by means of a brief discussion of what Orwell calls the *not un*-formation. We do not join Geoffrey Pullum in "Orwell and the Not Unblack Dog"[13] in characterizing Orwell's infamous footnote from "Politics and the English Language" as dishonest. We settle for calling that footnote a counterproductive distraction that we hope our students disregard. Whether Orwell's disparagements of the *not un*-formation are intellectually dishonest, merely sloppy, or pedantically sophistic matters little to us. Those disparagements detract from the coherence and cogency Orwell's essay. Orwell's vivid, concrete scorn provides Orwell's detractors and Orwell's admirers alike memorable overstatement to discuss, directing discussion from the weightier issues that Orwell claimed his essay concerned.

Orwell was correct to note that hackneyed understatement might enable political writers to evade clarity and precision in favor of intellectually pretentious but noncommittal phrasings.[14] If we say a presentation is not uninteresting, for example, we commit ourselves to minimal approval and may damn with faint praise (or be understood to damn with faint praise). That noncommittal appraisals are often polite or kind makes them no less evasive, we concede.

That much granted, we hold that Orwell took his protest too far—caricature risks such excesses—and attached to a common way of speaking and writing far more potency than it could possess even in theory. If he thought his trashing of the *not un-*formation through, he would admit that *not un-* often makes clearer and more honest what a political writer is arguing or claiming. Whenever a political writer elects not to think or write in absolute or categorical terms and instead admits to some wide range of possibilities, that writer disdains a false dichotomy in favor of a usually more accurate spectrum. Dimensional or dialectical writing, Orwell would have to admit, exhibits the very sincerity, open-mindedness, and avoidance of pat phrases that he advised repeatedly in his essay. Courts, for example, often find that a constitution neither mandates nor forbids some policy; when they are precise, such courts say the policy is not unconstitutional and leave matters there. For a second example, we two would have preferred that, at the time Orwell was writing and publishing his essay, more Americans could have understood that dissenters and leftists were not un-American.

Angered by prose devices he despised, Orwell mistook thoughtless or shameless deployment of those devices for symptoms, perhaps even causes (God help him and us!), of the death-spiral of politicking and writing he diagnosed. In his righteous indignation he took his readers on a hunt and for a ride. Readers, including students, likely remember the ride and the hunt if they recall the essay at all. They tend not to recall that their journey never turned up the wild goose, the snark, or the specter identified as a target in the beginning and end of "Politics and the English Language." Nor did they detect *corpus delecti* or other evidence of the wave of political or linguistic crimes from which Orwell begins and with which he ends.

Notes

1. We therefore violate Orwell's injunctions against Latinate jargon as well as one or more of his rules.
2. Please recall that in the essay Orwell characterizes ideologically orthodox prose in the manner that we two have. Please review words 3,433 through 3,713 at politicsandtheenglishlanguage.info/full.html or ¶ 12 in our telescoping diagram at politicsandtheenglishlanguage.info/telescope.html.
3. We two intend "Procurator" as a slur on Orwell's reprehensible prosecution of hapless innocents. Beyond the denotations of "procurator"—an official in Roman law regimes who acts as an administrative or financial agent or, more generally, an agent of an estate-holder or an emperor—lies the connotation of

"procurator" as an apparatchik in the former Soviet Union or an administrator in the Roman Empire whose activities hide behind a jural façade. Pontius Pilate is an example.

4. Still, Geoffrey Pullum is persuasive in arguing that Orwell's insistence on avoiding established metaphors is silly. "Elimination of the Fittest," *Lingua Franca* (blog), accessed April 4, 2013, www.chronicle.com/blogs/linguafranca/2013/04/04/elimination-of-the-fittest/.

5. We note from *Random House Unabridged Dictionary*, 2nd ed. (New York: Random House, 2010), 603, that the skipping of rocks across calm waters came to be called "ducks and drakes" in the 16th century. If that metaphor is not dead, it is Methuselah.

6. We are unsure that hackneyed phrases and dying metaphors have seemed apt over time else they would not be repeated, but we want our readers to consider that possibility.

7. We coauthors advise our students to revise, rethink, and proofread, but we do so less pedantically, we hope. We do so as well believing that propagandists and spinmeisters—"political writers" who threaten polities and languages far more than the writers Orwell roughs up—run their "prose" past focus groups and political operatives who will eliminate operators or verbal false limbs to maximize the effectiveness of genuine swindles and perversions. Dr. Frank Luntz, for example, has nearly made swindling citizens and perverting politics a science: Frank I. Luntz, *Words That Work: It's Not What You Say, It's What People Hear* [comma-splice as in published title] (New York: Hatchette Books, 2007).

8. Sharon Crowley, *Toward a Civil Discourse: Rhetoric and Fundamentalism* (Pittsburgh: University of Pittsburgh Press, 2006); Linda Kintz, "Clarity, Mothers, and the Mass-Mediated National Soul: A Defense of Ambiguity," in *Media, Culture, and the Religious Right*, eds. Linda Kintz and Julia Lesage (Minneapolis: University of Minnesota Press, 1998), 115–139; Nate Kreuter, "The Ethics of Clarity and/or Obscuration," *Composition Forum* 27 (2013): 18. See also Kathryn Flannery, *The Emperor's New Clothes: Literature, Literacy, and the Ideology of Style* (Pittsburgh: University of Pittsburgh Press, 1995).

9. See *Quote Investigator: Exploring the Origins of Quotations*, accessed August 25, 2017, https://quoteinvestigator.com/new-book/.

10. We do not know that it is worse that the sentence buries its main point at the end. If the sentence were prose and not verse and if the author were not divinely inspired, we should respectfully recommend inverting the sentence: "Because [the passage of] time and chance affect[s] us all, the swiftest may not win every race and the strongest may lose battles to the weaker."

11. Please note that, as with Professors Laski and Hogben, Orwell derides a style far more common in academia than in political writing.

12. We once again play off the sentence "I will come back to this presently, and I hope that by that time the meaning of what I have said here will have become clearer."

13. Pullum, "Elimination of the Fittest."

14. Orwell notes the *not un*-formation in two or three spots in his essay, depending on how one counts. Amid the sixth paragraph of his essay (by our count in our telescoping diagram; words 997–1011 in the word count at our website) Orwell scores the formation for its pretentiousness amid Orwell's discussion of operators or verbal false limbs: "banal statements are given an appearance of profundity by means of the *not un*-formation." In his 16th paragraph (by our

telescoping diagram's count; words 3979–3992 at our website) Orwell notes anew "it should also be possible to laugh the *not un*-formation out of existence," to which he attaches a footnote that offers his dig at once most memorable and most execrable: "One can cure oneself of the *not un*-formation by memorizing this sentence: *A not unblack dog was chasing a not unsmall rabbit across a not ungreen field.*"

Bibliography

Crowley, Sharon. *Toward a Civil Discourse: Rhetoric and Fundamentalism.* Pittsburgh: University of Pittsburgh Press, 2006.

Flannery, Kathryn. *The Emperor's New Clothes: Literature, Literacy, and the Ideology of Style.* Pittsburgh: University of Pittsburgh Press, 1995.

Kintz, Linda. "Clarity, Mothers, and the Mass-Mediated National Soul: A Defense of Ambiguity." In *Media, Culture, and the Religious Right*, edited by Linda Kintz and Julia Lesage, 115–139. Minneapolis: University of Minnesota Press, 1998.

Kreuter, Nate. "The Ethics of Clarity and/or Obscuration." *Composition Forum* 27 (2013): 18.

Luntz, Frank I. *Words That Work: It's Not What You Say, It's What People Hear.* New York: Hatchette Books, 2007.

Pullum, Geoffrey. "Elimination of the Fittest." *Lingua Franca* (blog), April 4, 2013. www.chronicle.com/blogs/linguafranca/2013/04/04/elimination-of-the-fittest/.

Pullum, Geoffrey. "Orwell and the Not Unblack Dog." *Lingua Franca* (blog), April 8, 2013. http://chronicle.com/blogs/linguafranca/2013/04/08/orwell-and-the-not-unblack-dog/.

Quote Investigator: Exploring the Origins of Quotations. Accessed August 25, 2017. https://quoteinvestigator.com/new-book/.

Random House Unabridged Dictionary. 2nd ed. New York: Random House, 2010.

5 Toward Habits of Discernment

Refurbishing Orwell's Lists
Amid Pseudocracy

In Chapter 1, we promised to review "Orwell's ballyhooed rules and buried questions" so as to explore the third, most specific irony we have concocted: Orwell's seldom-remembered questions promote far clearer, far more thoughtful writing than his often-recalled rules. In this chapter, we redeem our promise. We show that Orwell entombed his list of questions at the end of a very long paragraph but that those questions, disinterred, might encourage writers' capacities for discernment (what we label **attitude**) and for craft and even art in writing (what we label **aptitude**) far beyond the capacity of the list of rules that Orwell set apart and thereby enshrined. We then generalize such attitudes toward such aptitudes for listening to and reading mass-mediated discourses to secure productive habits of communication and cogitation. Orwell's attitudes and aptitudes, flowing into **habits** of mind, pen, or keyboard, are what we believe our students and other readers of "Politics and the English Language" ought to acquire.

In this chapter we reassess Orwell's lists in light of how people tend to learn to write and thereby to read. In 1945–46 Orwell was attempting to improve writing. The manner in which Orwell instructed readers of his essay seems to us two to follow more from Orwell's own training in composition than from what we regard as his signal contributions in the essay: his deconstruction of euphemisms and his interlinking of political and linguistic decadence to insincerity, orthodoxy, and deception. We think this explains at least partially Orwell's "Memorable Misdirection" in lists, especially his six rules that could remedy neither general political and linguistic decline nor particular political phrases yet have eclipsed Orwell's far more useful advice for students, readers, and writers. In contrast to Orwell's experiences in learning to write in his own style, we posit our experiences in teaching college students to write (and to read and to listen) amid the pseudocracy and post-literacy of the 21st-century United States. Our experiences include encouraging a perceptive, self-critical reflection complementary to the sardonic reactions and responses of Orwell (a.k.a., our Irony

Three), so our design in this chapter is to extract from Orwell's essay the sorts of **attitudes** (Chapter 3), **aptitudes** (Chapter 4), and **habits** (this chapter) that his essay might encourage in adults who read and write.[1] Those who argue vehemently for or against Orwell's three lists may have grasped Orwell's rules—even if they make little sense—but may not have taken them in the attitude that Orwell advised in paragraph 18 of his essay. This, our fifth chapter, concerns such attitudes behind Orwell's laws and lists more than the letter of his catalogue, his questions, and his rules. Our fifth chapter likewise considers the aptitudes that Orwell displayed in unmasking and debunking euphemisms devious and mind-numbing and in associating insincerity, orthodoxy, and deception with political and linguistic decadence in our times if not quite in his own. The attitudes and aptitudes that we claim to discern in Orwell's enterprise yield habits of reading and writing that, we argue, can at least improve our readers' communicating and may even enhance our readers' understanding and their resistance to bunk.

How Orwell Learned to Write *Versus* How Moderns Learn to Write

Orwell learned to write quite deliberately.[2] As early as age five or six, Orwell claimed, he determined to become a writer.[3] At a Catholic convent, then at St. Cyprian's School, and finally at Eton, he wrote and translated extensively in Greek and Latin, which may have informed if not formed his opinions regarding the gilding of modern English with classical patinas, the seasoning of stale rhetoric with ancient phrasings, or the padding of prose with pretentious derivations. Although of course he wrote compositions in English, more of his experience writing in his native language came from contributing to school newspapers and magazines than formal—and formulaic?—practice in classes. At Eton much of his output was satirical, perhaps prefiguring his parodies and novels. Whatever influences we may attribute to Orwell's formal schooling, we know of no classes he took in English composition and writing about literature in English, classes that became a staple of British and American education after World War Two.

Like most of us, then, Orwell learned to write by writing a lot, by developing his own tastes in prose style, and by defining his own way of writing in contrast to that of other writers. For example, he believed Henry Miller's style had "a fine rhythm," even as he believed American English was "less flexible and refined" than British English but had more vigor. Orwell thought Ezra Pound was "a ferocious pedant" (which might explain Orwell's first three specimens), preferred Housman's and Kipling's verse to Modernist poetry (which we might associate with Orwell's concerns for economy and rhythm), and believed Dylan Thomas's poetry "too rhetorical," an assessment that may unwittingly reveal Orwell's attitude toward rhetoric, as if the latter were a matter only of flourishes, decoration, and bombast.

One of his biographers, George Bowker, recalls an anecdote from Orwell's friend, Michael Sayers, who "came across Orwell one day writing in his room" (in the 1930s, after Orwell had begun to publish widely). Orwell was reading passages from Jonathan Swift's *A Modest Proposal* and W. Somerset Maugham, closing the books, and copying sentences from memory. Sayers recalled that one of Orwell's aims was "to find a [prose] style which eliminates the adjective,"[4] an aim that might exemplify Orwell's preference for concreteness and against abstractions in his 1946 essay.

Orwell's compulsive, perhaps even Puritanical drive to trim prose (Rule iii: "If it is possible to cut a word out, always cut it out") and his packaging of disparate elements of writing (paragraph-breaks, specific choices among words in favor of shorter over longer, simplification of style) into an ethic of composition seem rather idiosyncratic and severe. We concede that Orwell learned some of his preferences for and in writing in formal settings, but we wonder to what degree Orwell acquired his doctrinaire predilections in a less systematic, more self-willed manner than we might expect in the US and UK these days. We do not claim that we can align any of Orwell's lists with either his formal or his self-directed training. Rather, we contend that Orwell came by his pronouncements concerning the English language less communally and more individually or individualistically than many writers then or most writers now. We do not wonder, it follows, that Orwell's approach to rhetoric and writing was, as we have noted in previous chapters, spotty and dotty.

Orwell's self-willed, self-made style may explain why in "Politics and the English Language" he never explored genre. Orwell leaves his readers either to assume that he may be discussing *belles lettres*[5] or to admit that they do not know even approximately what kind of writing he has in mind. The essay does not address genre and its effects on style. It is common knowledge that style and diction, among other things, change with every genre of writing, so that, for example, to warn writers away from jargon, as Orwell did, does not make sense for someone writing an academic essay, technical report, or even an expert's opinion in a periodical or on a website. We know you can envisage how you would change your writing when you moved from one distinct genre to another.

We agree heartily with Orwell that the authors of the five specimens of what he thought to be bad writing might productively have asked themselves if more revision were required. But if the five authors judged their prose to be at least adequate for the purposes and audiences for which and for whom they were writing, they might have decided that the job was done. That is, they may have decided that what Orwell concluded was pretentious or jargon-laced diction suited their audiences and purposes. Obviously, audience should not excuse everything. Full-time propagandists who do not fall into their own traps write for an audience they hope is composed almost entirely of suckers. That the audience is thusly composed does not excuse the propagandists for the cynical, even depraved, choices they make when they write. Similarly, when academic writers indulge in difficulty to make their topic more complex than it is, the fault lies with them, not their audience.

Now we will briefly contrast Orwell's formal schooling, self-instruction, and invention of his own tastes and distastes with how writing is taught in high schools, colleges, and universities nowadays. Because our views of writing spring from our own educations, our experiences in classrooms, what we know of other college teachers, and developments in the field of rhetoric-and-composition, the comparison will help show why we critique the essay and its lists the way we do and how we shall make Orwell work nowadays.

Strikingly absent from Orwell's essay is any significant discussion of at least three key elements of traditional rhetoric—audience, purpose, and process—on which Aristotle lectured amid the 300s BCE and which have guided composition for centuries. He defined past-oriented rhetoric as *forensic* (what really happened?) and future-oriented rhetoric *deliberative* (what ought we to do, given the circumstances?). Aristotle also sketched a process whereby one arrived at one's topic; he called it "invention" (*inventio* is the Latin term, *heuresis* the Greek).[6] We know such heuristic processes now as research, investigation, brainstorming, drafting, and so on. Is it unlikely that any short list of rules or questions or cavils about swindles and perversions could cover such varied processes, purposes, and audiences?

Nor do Orwell's lists of words, phrases, or other particulars address construction of arguments at any higher level that students must master if they are to participate in political or other discourses. As Edward P.J. Corbett has explained in *Classical Rhetoric for the Modern Student*, writers must invent arguments by making strategic and tactical decisions about what kinds of appeal to make to an audience: rational (*logos*), emotional (*pathos*), and/ or arguments from the authority or credibility of the rhetor (*ethos*).[7] In this context, use of passive voice or "false verbal limbs" would be a lesser concern. Orwell's focus on piecemeal composition yielded relatively positive questions and relatively negative rules that do not speak to the more momentous concerns of writers, especially those who are learning to write a century after Orwell taught himself to write.

Modern teachers of composition instruct students to conceive of producing prose as a process; "Politics and the English Language" reads as if Orwell directed writers to sit down, to contemplate wordlessly, and only then to hurl themselves at word-choices and phrase-making, keeping in mind some bits of advice and thereby to producing something quickly and directly that improved on common writing.

We find it difficult to overstate differences between the crabbed understanding of writing that Orwell taught himself and then imparted in his essay and capacious conceptions of writing with which modern students are regaled and, sometimes, entertained or informed or even instructed.

But in this chapter, we are long overdue in giving Orwell his due. Even if we view Orwell's essay through the lens of contemporary ideas of writing-instruction, we may reinterpret his admonishments, lists, and rules as an attempt to instill more self-conscious **attitudes** in writers. As noted, contemporary writing-instruction attempts to build such self-consciousness in students. But in his own way, Orwell was attempting to instill in writers more alert habits of mind—at least implicitly and, we think, explicitly. We may quibble with this or that rule, admonishment, or predilection, but the bigger picture is that Orwell encouraged writers to be aware and to be wary, to adopt an attitude of vigilance and to cultivate an aptitude for targeted, sensible skepticism for which, in Chapter 3, we praised those who systematically assess claims, arguments, and presumptions of authorities and celebrities. Perhaps more indirectly than we two think, Orwell encourages writers to write less automatically and not to fall into a kind of semi-conscious, distracted writing that is inordinately vulnerable to clichés, unnecessary jargon, dead metaphors, and other potential symptoms of half-hearted effort or autopilot writing. Maybe he meant to invite writers to be among their own toughest critics.

If Orwell was advocating vigilance as attitude and demonstrating his own aptitude for skepticism, his three lists—his catalogue, his questions, and his rules—seem ill-chosen. Please consider his catalogue first. Can you imagine constructing a perfectly loathsome, unsupportable argument in writing that contains no dying metaphors, no "verbal false limbs," not a hint of pretentious diction, and no "meaningless" words? So can we. More to the point, so can politicos who write clear, simple "copy," albeit for manipulative, nefarious reasons or causes. Reflect on most of the political-campaign "arguments" you are asked to consider, via television, the Internet, radio, or print. Regardless of party affiliation and regardless of what policy, real or imagined, might be at stake, don't you find many of these "well written" compared to Orwell's "catalogue" or Orwell's "specimens?" Aren't fund-raising emails from political campaigns terse, effective, and otherwise well written? Don't we expect sound bites on broadcast media to be calculated and crafted to deceive without resort to any of the swindles and perversions that Orwell catalogued? In other words, writers of advertising copy and nightly news not only may avoid the sins in Orwell's first list—his catalogue—but also must avoid such failings routinely if they are to partici-pate in and to profit from the decline of English owing to the vicious effect of politics.

Nonetheless, Orwell's catalogue is instructive if writers apply the listed lessons in due time and at due scale and, more important, if they derive from the catalogue Orwellian **attitude** against vagueness, equivocation, and decep-tion. If writers reconsider would-have-been swindles and perversions—and, far more common, prose that says far less than or nearly the opposite of what the writers intended to write—as they produce second, perhaps even third, drafts that they still regard as preliminary, then with good intentions they may not further the decline of politicking and of language. If such writers make a **habit** of policing multiple drafts, alerted by Orwell to some sloppiness and sleight-of-hand common in and since 1945, then writers and perhaps readers will improve their abilities to spot and to scorn swindles and perversions and deceptions and nonsense.

Near the end of his paragraph regarding "meaningless words" Orwell hit his stride. He provided examples of truly perverse, truly deceitful uses of language that might degrade the polity. Orwell paraded words almost emp-tied of meaning beyond their power to slur ("Fascism"), ambiguous praises and smears ("democracy" and "socialism" for instance), equivocations deployed to please an audience while permitting the deployer a private, plausible deniability, and other attempts to deceive with shifty language.

We agree with Orwell that these abuses of language may swindle or per-vert the unwary reader and perhaps the unwary writer. We stubbornly insist, however, that his listing gets in the way of these telling instances. And—Irony Three again—his catalogue and its four labels are recalled far more often than his most convincing particulars. Those particulars demonstrate Orwell's skill at revealing truly political usages and his manner of confront-ing truly degrading and truly disgraceful use of language—a skill and a manner that we find lacking throughout the rest of his catalogue of cheats and cons. That skill and manner follow from **attitudes** we should have our students acquire from "Politics and the English Language" and may inspire **aptitudes** for critical reading and writing.

In sum, Orwell's self-instruction in the English language, as opposed to how high schools and colleges teach English in the 21st century, 1) at least partly explains his focus on gibes and gripes, and 2) at least partly explains why he paraded punctilious trivialities that got in the way of weightier attitudes and habits that Orwell might better have displayed and thereby inculcated in the writers whom he explicitly targeted and the readers whom we instructors send to Orwell's essay. Whatever the explanation, List One abounds in fussy, fusty pedantry that yields late-draft, piecemeal shalt-nots almost to the exclusion of positive **attitudes**, **aptitudes**, and **habits** that would better inform early-draft, holistic writing as well as late-draft, piece-meal editing.

Orwell's Second List—Questions Scrupulous Writers Ask Themselves Hint at Attitudes and Aptitudes If Not at Habits

Orwell's second list provides writers and readers alike questions that vary in their utility for early drafts and for holistic or strategic writing but at least cover some of the **attitudes**, **aptitudes**, and **habits** that we two treasure in his essay.

The second list appears at the end of a long paragraph (¶11 in our tele-scoping diagram) in which he summarizes his case against modern, written English and skewers anew Professor Laski and the other alleged miscreants guilty of committing modern, decadent English in the five specimens:

> A scrupulous writer, in every sentence that he writes, will ask himself at least four questions, thus: 1. What am I trying to say? 2. What words will express it? 3. What image or idiom will make it clearer? 4. Is this image fresh enough to have an effect? And he will probably ask himself two more: 1. Could I put it more shortly? 2. Have I said anything that is avoidably ugly?[8]

The questions themselves may be fine ones for writers to ask themselves as they write,[9] but, as we have noted above with regard to Orwell's catalogue of swindles and perversions, some of these are even finer if asked at an appropriate stage and setting in the writing (and, neglected by Orwell in his "informal" and rushed essay, the revising and redrafting).

Question One—"What Am I Trying to Say?"

Almost all writers will ask themselves this question, and those who do not probably have problems far more troubling—modern teachers of writing would say, of a far higher order[10]—than choices among words (the question Orwell put second on his list), fresh images or vivid idioms (questions three and four combined), concision (Question Five), or avoidable ugliness (Orwell's last question—an aesthetic one). "What am I trying to say?" is a recurring question because writers tend to revise not only their prose but their opinions and aims—sometimes even their purposes and their attitudes toward their own prose—as they write and rewrite. Were we to lapse into jargon derived from ancient Greek, we should claim that Orwell's first question is often but not always *architectonic* and *dialectical*, by which we mean that "What am I trying to say?" shapes or guides other questions and answers to other questions even as answers to the other questions reshape the answers to "What am I trying to say?" (*Architectonic*). That question and answers carom back and forth throughout drafting (*Dialectical*).

One virtue of that first question seems evident: Answering it overcomes the indifference to meaning, to expression, and to effect that Orwell listed as a common bad habit in the specimens he ridiculed. He ascribed commonly poor prose to writers' indifference to precise and fresh expression and even a lack of sufficient interest in what the writer was writing and in how the writer was arguing. Whatever our cavils about the first question, then, he advises writers well to attend to their overarching point or points repeatedly, consistently, even doggedly. The question, moreover, pertains directly to his diagnosis of prose maladies across the political and linguistic systems and sentence by sentence. Writers who develop the call for candor implicit in Question One (**attitude**) into practiced alacrity at addressing Question One forthrightly and completely (**aptitude**) likely develop **habits** of honest, guileless expression. The first question will avail readers and consumers of media at every stage as well.

Question Two—"What Words Will Express It?"

Orwell's second question, "What words will express it?" even imports answers to the first question as the antecedent of "it." Writers answer this second question by selecting the words, phrases, clauses, sentences, and paragraphs they believe will best express what writers are trying to say (and thereby answer Orwell's first question). Every writer, unscrupulous or scrupulous, in the process of writing repeatedly asks and answers Orwell's second question. Scrupulous writers may include "best" or some other modifier for "express" lest they set too low their standard for their writing. Answers to Question Two will change amid and across drafts, however. As what an author is trying to say shifts as part of the back and forth connected to Orwell's first question, the best way to express what the author is trying to say must change accordingly. Moreover, the words that might, in the abstract, best express what the author is trying to say may evolve with prior and subsequent answers to Question Two. A stark phrasing or vivid rendering in one passage may and probably should alter phrasings or renderings elsewhere. Repeating the single best expression of what the writer means to say will get stale soon. And, as we have stressed, the words, phrases, and clauses that will best express what the writer is trying to say will most concern the writer to varying degrees at varying stages in composition, so Orwell might have improved on this second question by referring explicitly to second and third drafts and recommending implicitly the redrafting and rethinking that Orwell's essay could have used. Still, his fierce **attitudes** of utmost candor and relentless clarity and his **aptitude** for unfaltering emphasis on the concrete illuminate his second question. They may even lead writers and readers to cultivate **habits** of precision in expression.

Question Three—"What Image or Idiom Will Make It Clearer?"

We trust that Orwell's third question anticipated revision and redrafting, else we must ask, "Clearer than what?" Please note that this question, like the second one, imports Orwell's first question (the antecedent of "it"). We wish Orwell had not restricted his question to idiom and image; logic, statistics, analogies, allusions, examples, brief narratives, expositions, syllogisms, and references to authorities might clarify writing and reveal to writers what they had not seen before they started writing.

Orwell's third question is apt advice in general and in particular resonates with his complaints about vagueness and imprecision in modern writing, especially tactical nebulousness and practiced woolliness in political writing (**attitude**), even if that question stops short of counseling writers to acquire other tools and practices that might improve specific communications and collective discourse (**aptitude**). Readers and writers alike should consistently demand precision and clarity in what they read and write, so the third question, extracted from a nearly endless paragraph and drilled as a **habit** for reading and writing, will avail 21st-century communicators.

Question Four—"Is This Image Fresh Enough to Have an Effect?"

If writers are trying to persuade an audience by means of image, then the fresher the image, the better. Other times, a pre-owned phrase like "putting the cart before the horse" (for example) may inform readers efficiently and effectively. Freshness versus familiarity depends on audience, purpose, genre, and context, so writers had better be selective in answering Orwell's fourth question as in acting upon answers, and readers had better not demand novel coinages at some cost in clarity, precision, or other demands of Orwell's prior questions. Earlier in the essay, Orwell allowed as how dead metaphors are sometimes acceptable, so that the emphasis in this list on fresh idioms and images might perplex some readers of the essay. In the matter of Question Four, then, his penchant for striking prose with vivid images may undermine his preference for clarity and concreteness.

Question Five—"Could I Put It More Shortly?"

Question Five must serve writers better than Rule iii: "If it is possible to cut a word out, always cut it out." With qualification and elaboration, the fifth question may serve writers well. Its utility will depend in part on a writer's **habits** of drafting and editing, and communicators should, in keeping with Orwell's repeated exhortations, sacrifice some concision to achieve greater clarity.

Question Six—Have I Said Anything That Is Avoidably Ugly?

Once readers recall that Orwell had already inscribed that "[t]he English language becomes ugly and inaccurate because our thoughts are foolish, but the slovenliness of our language makes it easier for us to have foolish thoughts," they should understand him to mean that ugly usage and ugly prose were avoidable only with the "necessary first step" of identifying and eliminating slovenly language. Should one read Question Six to prefer aesthetics—prettiness, the opposite of ugliness—to logic, evidence, authority, or other virtues not explicit in Orwell's questions? That is, this question seems to concern decorum, inside knowledge, and what "just isn't done."

The final question becomes more understandable if we keep in mind that some kinds of prose bothered Orwell to a degree that many of us in the 21st century may not share. The bothersome kinds of prose seem to share pretentiousness, abstraction, and pomp and to lack sufficient vigor or directness or, God help Orwell and the rest of us, manliness. Orwell manages to typify as ugly kinds of prose or stylings that he doesn't produce. To the degree that Question Six concerns what makes his prose better than the prose in his five specimens, avoiding ugliness may not have helped writers much in 1946 and may assist writers and readers even less decades later.[11]

An implication of Question Six may matter greatly for writers and readers, however. Unlike its predecessors, it presumes that writers assess after writing. Even if Question Six directs the scrupulous writer upon completion of each conscientious sentence to look back for ugliness that might be avoidable, such an attitude is better than no proofreading and no redrafting at all, even as it may make the writing process halting.[12]

The spirit of these questions is part of what makes Orwell's essay usefully portable to our century and the era of pseudocracy. Soon we shall discuss why we hold this view, but first we must discuss a third list.

His Third List—Orwell's Ill-Phrased Rules Fritter Away the Attitudes and Aptitudes That His More Useful Questions Might Bequeath

Say what we dare about Orwell's list of six questions that scrupulous writers ask themselves, we find that list far superior to the list of six rules that, Orwell claims, "will cover most cases" when "instinct" fails to inform writers about which words or phrases to choose to achieve the effect writers desire. We have indicated that his rules, in our experience, are recalled far more often than his questions. His setting his six rules apart from his main text while he buried his six questions might account for the greater renown of his rules. Also, the rules came after the questions and so might supplant them in the mind of the reader. For whatever reasons, Orwell's rules have outshone his questions.

We now make bold to proclaim that Orwell's six rules epitomize Irony Three far beyond the impact of his catalogue or his questions. In the 21st century if not in 1946, the rules have eclipsed more useful advice for students, readers, and writers. Orwell's small-scale, memorable misdirection detracted from his skillful exposure of euphemisms, insincerity, orthodoxy, and deceptions that he proclaimed rampant. To the degree that his memorable misdirection distracted and continues to distract incautious readers from his far more edifying, far more prophylactic, and far less punctilious attitudes and aptitudes, too many readers likely take from "Politics and the English Language" less instruction than they might.

Hence, while all three lists, in our assessment, detract and distract from the attitudes, aptitudes, and habits that we deem most valuable in Orwell's classic (whence Irony Three), the third and final list, the concluding set of rules, is the most forcefully stated, as Orwell signaled by his use of "Never" four times and "always" once. He played Moses to turn advice into commandments. That this third and final list is the best known makes it to us the most bothersome. That he propounded the list in such absolutes makes it to us his most perilous tactic.

Thus, our major difficulty with Orwell's listed rules is less that he dashed them off (and thereby bungled his phrasing of the rules—see earlier chapters) and more that his rules betray his admirable **attitudes** and demonstrated **aptitudes** and, in the unlikely eventuality that a writer adhered to the list of six rules, instill in writers counterproductive **habits**. Let us proceed rule by rule to meet our burden.

Rule i—"Never Use a Metaphor, Simile, or Other Figure of Speech Which You Are Used to Seeing in Print."

Perhaps to make his first rule seem commanding, Orwell left "thoughtlessly" out of his first rule. We would prefer the rule to read "Never thoughtlessly traffick in metaphors, similes, or other figures of speech which you are used to seeing in print." We have noted that, depending upon the rhetorical situation in which one finds oneself, metaphors, similes, or other figures of speech that one is used to seeing in print may prove advantageous. Catchphrases, slogans, and some other words and phrases are designed to be repeated, for example. Sound bites are selected for making sense instantly.

Our most serious problem with Rule i is that Orwell's pithy stringency and pretended certitude shout down both **attitudes** that Orwell displayed that might better avail writers and **aptitudes** that he demonstrated in arguing his case. We have already formulated as "critical discernment" a set of attitudes that imbue "Politics and the English Language" and inform his first commandment. We have also described a corresponding set of aptitudes as among the greatest virtues of "Politics and the English Language" and among the greatest skills he evinced: ferreting out meaningless trafficking in second-hand phrases and hackneyed allusions. When he regales readers who are writers with mindless, perhaps eyeless oratorical automatons dispensing platitudes intended to numb minds, we marvel at his essay.

Rule ii—"Never Use a Long Word When a Short One Will Do."

Is Orwell's second exhortation the silliest of all Orwell's rules? Choosing a five-letter word that expresses meaning adequately—which is what we take Orwell to have meant when he settled for "will do"—over a ten-letter word that seems perfectly apt would be the easy, lazy manner of writing against which he explicitly set himself, so that cannot be what he meant. But that is what he wrote. This second rule, read and applied as published in 1946, contradicts his advice to let meaning choose the best word(s) rather than to let the words direct the meaning. Not only does he command writers to let the words determine the meaning, but he also mandates that the length of the words should make the determination.

The greater folly of Orwell's second formulation is that it likely distracts readers from his excoriations of grandiloquent, polysyllabic bombast and puffery. Throughout the essay, Orwell riotously lampoons pretense and pretentiousness in favor of straightforward, candid expression. That is an **attitude** we hope students and other writers pick up from the classic. We fear, however, that he hides this important, constructive, high-minded attitude behind bold ukases[13] that he does not mean but lists. Not only does his second item get in the way of his modeling of an important attitude, but it also threatens to interfere with his talent for and skill in applying that attitude. Orwell's aptitude for puncturing pretense is a priceless gift, especially to high school or college beginners relatively new to assessing writing critically. Instead, the rule infotains more than informs and risks misinforming.

Rule iii—"If It Is Possible to Cut a Word Out, Always Cut It Out."

As noted earlier, this rule traps Orwell's essay in contradictions and absurdities. The absurd contradictions of Rule iii are not, however, its gravest shortcomings for readers and writers. More grave in our view is that it eclipses Orwell's worthy reproaches against padding prose, especially with words or phrases selected to impress or to pretend to authority or acumen that writers do not possess or should not be accorded. His youthful flirtation with excising adjectives having given way to middle-aged fervor to cut whatever might be cut, Orwell amid his essay stressed the cutting of words or phrases that added little beyond length or rhythm. This ethos of economy and elegance informed his prose often in the essay when he demonstrated his adeptness at selecting just the right word; candid, even stark phrasings; and, most important, concrete expression.

Rule iv—"Never Use the Passive Where You Can Use the Active [Voice]."

Rule iv reduces the writer's toolbox to one of the two grammatical voices in English and (maybe) leaves authors to versions of the verb to be. We have also noted that "where you can use the active" is a nearly null proviso because all English verbs that admit of a passive voice possess an active voice. The only reason Orwell supplies for diminishing tools in the writer's toolbox is to prevent writers or speakers from hiding responsibility or agency for decisions or actions, but many, perhaps most, uses of the passive voice do not dodge blame but merely state facts and opinions straightforwardly with less emphasis on agents or agency than on other aspects. (If, as a cliché as dead as Caesar claims, "the die is cast," it may not matter by whom.) Thus, if he wanted perpetually to caution writers against obscuring agency, he might have heeded his own advice and written candidly "Do not hide agents." Beyond that useful advice, writers should use active and passive voices with the judgment and discretion Orwell counsels and practices himself.

Rule v—"Never Use a Foreign Phrase, a Scientific Word, or a Jargon Word If You Can Think of an Everyday English Equivalent."

Rule v might be more helpful to readers who overlook the directive Orwell dashed off in favor of what he himself said and did elsewhere in his essay. We think he strove for precision and denounced vagueness, sought concreteness and denounced fancy and fantasy, and preferred honesty to guile. He applied the foregoing attitudes with alacrity throughout his essay. Who could fail to see Orwell's delight in exposing mind-numbing euphemisms and mindless orthodoxies, partisan hackery and ideological butchery, and other dark arts by which liars made lies seem truthful and murderers made murders respectable, even heroic? In our view, then, Rule v supplies not very helpful counsel that supplants truly edifying examples of the attitudes and aptitudes that are the essay's great gift.

Rule vi—"Break Any of These Rules Sooner Than Say Anything Outright Barbarous."

Orwell's Rule vi does not quite say "Forget every item above" but comes close. Moreover, "barbarous" is often a matter of taste: Neither Orwell's lists nor his examples reveal what kind of prose might be less ugly or less barbarous unless the passive voice and "scientific words" are, by definition, ugly and barbarous. (If they are, then further confusion ensues.) Earlier we suggested why Orwell cannot be clearer about barbarism and ugliness in writing: his neglect of context, purpose, and audience. Thus, we cannot fairly task him for failing to define "barbarisms" in general. Absent a definition of "outright barbarism," however, Orwell's escape clause in Rule vi remains elusive if not useless.

We do not supply here the attitudes and aptitudes that Orwell might better have expressed in lieu[14] of Rule vi. If we are correct with regard to his first five rules, a reformulated sixth rule would be needless. The attitudes and aptitudes that Orwell demonstrated dramatically and repeatedly incorporate discernment, deliberation, and other forms of critical judgment, so ugliness and barbarism should be avoided by practice of the arts he advocated. We claim, in sum, that if his famed, defective rules were de-listed in favor of his evident practices, sober disposition, or critical temperament, his readers would be less tempted to try to adhere to vague invocations of "outright barbarous" or "ugly" or other unhelpful descriptors.

Effective Habits

To the extent that we have been at all persuasive thus far in this chapter, better lessons that readers might derive from "Politics and the English Language" are overdue. If Orwell's fussy, misguided, and misguiding lists of rules and japes do not suffice, what must readers of his classic learn, and what habits might they derive from his attitudes and aptitudes to enhance their own writing and reading?

When politics and other forces conspire to encourage mindlessness in writers and readers, Orwell's asserting mindfulness might encourage better writing, speaking, and reading. Most readers who have taken the essay seriously or have studied it as part of a course on writing probably have absorbed important points and pointers about discernment, judgment, awareness, and critical reading of one's own work and that of others. Even Orwell's fiercer critics, perhaps especially vehement detractors of "Politics and the English Language," ought to acknowledge as much.

We have derived from the essay habitual answers to questions that range from higher-order, global concerns with mindfulness to lower-order, local concerns more important when the larger designs of a writing have been executed:

Start From Honest Purposes and Reconcile Honorable Ends With Evolving Drafting—and Demand Authors You Read Do the Same

Orwell's attitude of candor and his aptitude for exposing pretense suggest that writers should ask themselves first, last, and at all times in between "For what honorable, honest purpose am I writing?" Indeed, we might designate this the "master question" that emerges from the essay's classic evisceration of pretense and prevarication. Directly following from and reinforcing that master question is "What am I presuming, implying, asserting, describing, telling, arguing, or explaining that is consistent with my own honor and honesty and that of my audience?" As writers adopt the **habit** of starting from honest purposes and reconciling honorable ends with evolving writing, and as they candidly inventory their turns of phrase and tropes to be certain that the particulars of the emerging writing comport with the writer's answers to the master question, writers must anticipate audience: "For whom am I writing, and what do they expect of me **consistent with honor and honesty**?" We do not enumerate these questions because they must always be informing one another as writers proceed. Listing would not adequately describe the dialectics of questions and of writing and reading. Rather, we two celebrate honest, honorable writing and reading by deriving from "Politics and the English Language" a "Master Habit" of the self-conscious candor and fairness that Orwell advocated.

Choose Straightforward, Respectable, and Guileless Phrasings and Figures That Might Approximate the Lofty Aspirations of Orwell for Conscientious Writing [and Reading]

While asking and answering larger-scale questions associated with the "Master Habit," writers should, on a smaller scale,

- question repeatedly how the organization or logic of their developing writing serves a well-meaning, aboveboard agenda;
- establish that any specialized language is at once appropriate to honest purposes and superior to less esoteric expression; and
- assure themselves that modes of expression (figures of speech and characterizations of opponents' claims, for examples) appeal to the virtues rather than the vulnerabilities of readers.

Let higher-order **habits** of writing with honesty, honor, and other lofty aspirations inform lower-order, later-in-writing-processes **habits** of maintaining the straightforward, appropriate, and guileless choices of phrasings and figures that might approximate the lofty aspirations.

Alienate Your Own Subjectivity; or, Watch What You're Doing

Amid higher-order, earlier drafting and lower-order, later refining alike, writers should when practicable anticipate readers from whom to elicit responses to and criticisms of developing drafts. Think how much Orwell might have improved his informal, precipitous essay if friends or critics had called him on some of the nonsense he dashed off! Readers often outstrip writers in honesty, in honorableness, and in exposing presumptions, implications, assertions, and innuendo that writers may have hidden from themselves. When such critics are not available, writers must assume the role of friendly but candid readers of their own writings. Both through friends, critics, and editors and through reading their own writing as if it were the writing of another, writers will emulate Orwell's fierce attitudes and scathing aptitudes by cultivating **habits** of "alienating their own subjectivity," more colloquially expressed as "watch what you're doing."

Expect Yourself to Succumb Anew to Your Own Vices as a Writer

The questions and habits above might alleviate high-order, "global" concerns or intermediate-order, "local" concerns as writers develop drafts, but when drafts seem complete or nearly so, writers must become even fiercer critics of their drafting or polishing. "Where does this draft deceive, pretend, mislead, rush, or fail?" "How might I correct any bits of writing that produce or threaten to produce confusion, credulity, or mindlessness?" Perhaps the most important **habit** to be promoted the further writers proceed into drafts is to repeatedly ask against which bad practices, lowly proclivities, and ignoble propensities writers should be always vigilant. "What questions must I ask myself, based upon my history as a writer?" That is, the discernment that Orwell encourages may be most effective when personalized.

The Pseudocracy Still Looms

Training ourselves in good habits based in Orwell's aptitudes and attitudes combined with questions that (self)-improving writers ask themselves about audiences, purposes, stages in composition, and the like may ward off some of the corroding effects of the "politics and economics" on which Orwell blamed the downward spiral of English in his first two paragraphs. But what of the politics and economics in which we read and write today? No matter how alert, self-critical, and sincere **producers** of messages may be, pseudocracy may prevail because **consumers** of discourse may not be equipped to handle what politics does to discourse. Even if we can handle the truth in most cases, we might not be able to handle the truthiness. Consequently, we recommend the following **habits** to people who read, watch, and listen to media, and who act upon politically affected discourse in the 21st century.

We now turn from production (writing) to consumption (reading, viewing, listening).

Politics had vitiated language in particulars, Orwell asserted, and we have insisted that his gibes and gripes constitute a list of abuses of language a bit too particular to him, his self-taught habits in writing, and his peculiar prejudices. Beyond his particulars, we have pursued ways in which politics corrupts language and language has corrupted politicking more generally. We claim to have isolated from Orwell's essay dispositions, capacities, and routines that we might infer from or insinuate into the essay. Now we will try to suggest by what habits writers and readers might protect their own communication against some effects of corruptions of politics and language.

Expect and Distrust Propaganda

Twenty-first-century communicators and especially consumers should avoid the ease of thinking that enemies or opponents or other fallen "theys" use propaganda but some "we, the better sort" do not. To believe that others resort to propaganda but we do not is shoddy, sloppy thinking rampant across religious disputation, nationalistic jingoism, racist cynicism, and other ideological conflicts that, in self-regarding moments, we pride ourselves on being above. Indeed, if you think of a political party as "yours," you likely suffer an effect of partisan propaganda and electoral imagery. So vital to the body politic have propagandizing and imagery become that, regardless of the politics, the culture, the nation, or the élites, you likely crave in your weaker moments a sense of belonging to some causes or crusades—at least until the "revolution" or "campaign" goes awry, when you will de-emphasize identifying yourself with the losing cause and resume your identification with another crusade. Propaganda is a permanent feature of modern politicking, governing, social media, and everyday conversation. In the modern pseudocracy, propagandas surround us each and all. Thus, we must distrust many sources of certainty. As consumers of communications, we must be reasonable, rational skeptics. Consistent with some of Orwell's finest virtues of thought and action, that virtue has become even more important since Orwell loosed his attitudes and aptitudes upon the 1930s and 1940s.

Cultivate Skepticism, Even Cynicism, About Mass Media; Avoid Being Enthralled to Current Events

Cultivated skepticism in an era of pervasive propaganda and continual pseudocracy is necessary for producers and consumers who would not race headlong into traps, but skepticism toward nations, causes, élites, and other collectivities is not sufficient. Thoroughgoing distrust of mass-mediated politicking and governing is another habit that sophisticated consumers of images and messages must acquire and hone. Even ineffective propaganda surrounds targeted populations with coordinated, systematic conditioning that mass media disseminate as information.[15] Citizens who would be current in a 24/7 news culture opt, often unknowingly, for infotaining propaganda: "heroes vs. villains" frames, shibboleths and slanders, and other corruptions that follow from an individual's becoming a "current events maven." Orchestrated messaging implants in psyches images and impressions that will widely persist even after fact-checkers debunk them. It follows that political image-making and myth-making is, at the very least, repeated, repackaged, and echoed in corporately centralized media whether images and myths spring from political marketing or from advertising.

Strive to Contextualize and to Systematize Rather Than to Individuate or to Particularize Whenever It Makes Sense to Do So

Yes, that is a mouthful, but here is what we are getting at: Orwell aggregated missteps he deemed "beneath" writers competent enough to command wide audiences or do substantial damage to English. Professor Laski's multiple negatives amid an abstruse critique of John Milton, Professor Hogben's dueling clichés in an obscure monograph, and the menace of false operators, jargon, and the like in pamphlets or newspapers were in the mid-20th century and are in the 21st century humbugs. All of us have predilections to attribute corruptions of communications to some viciousness we ascribe to others the better to transform opponents in a fair contest into enemies in an apocalyptic struggle between good and evil. Talk radio, cable television, and websites routinely villainize or even demonize individuals and lionize "us" in one form or another, to one degree or another. Those who acquire discerning attitudes and train target their aptitudes well will disdain (mis) characterizations of individuals precisely because if one or a few bad actors were the problem, "the problem" would not be systematic no matter how fancy our aggregating gripes or cavils.

Avoiding misdirected individuation, then, is another **habit** that we recommend to readers and writers who would emulate Orwell's most praiseworthy attitudes and aptitudes. When we find ourselves or others individuating, personalizing, scapegoating, or otherwise trivializing linguistic or rhetorical "offenses," we demand especially of ourselves but also of others evidence that vilification or demonization of a misstep is worthy of our or others' communicating. We may rephrase this habit in a somewhat more positive manner: Select your reading from and direct your communicating to subjects that most merit discerning, disciplined communication.[16]

Accommodate Multivalence

At their best, readers and writers nimbly negotiate not just "both sides" [AMBIvalence] but many sides [MULTIvalence]. To be their best, readers and writers must habitually put themselves in many shoes, pardon the familiar metaphor. They must recoil from fallacious "either/or" arguments. They must acknowledge sentiments and opinions contrary to their own presumptions and then state the worthiest countervailing considerations as persuasively as they can. Our suggesting that readers and writers develop such a habit may startle or alarm in an era saturated with propaganda on and from all sides and polarized venues in which assent to misinformation, even nonsense, is a "trained incapacity."[17] But in the context of this book and of Orwell's **attitudes** [especially antipathy to one-sided prattle] and **aptitudes** [especially his alacrity at exposing cunning euphemisms], we are obliged to recommend habits of cultivating contradictions and contrary views.

To train yourself in your reading and in your writing to cultivate multivalence(s), you must expect yourself to learn and to rethink as you read or write. At least entertain anew perspectives with which you have automatically or reflexively disagreed. Determine to encounter perspectives that you habitually have not even perceived. Evaluate evidence and logic that both novel (at least to you) and familiar viewpoints present. Exercise a contrarian will, and insist that every argument earn its keep even if—especially if—it springs from a way of thinking that ordinarily appeals to you. Why? Well, your mental muscles, like ours, could use the workout. Also, propagandists target you based on your habitual agreements and disagreements. They loathe skeptics and contrarians (unless propagandists are working for the Contrarian Convention). Infotainers play you for a sucker. Suckers never entertain opposing arguments. Don't be a sucker: Open your mind as you read and write and change your mind in mid-sentence if you find yourself doubting your own honesty or honorableness.

Make it your habit and even your hobby to be especially skeptical of sources that appeal to your usual ways of thinking. Presume that those with whom you agree are taking you for granted and are counting on your falling (again!) for the propagandistic two-step: Appeal to the masses but make every individual feel special.[18]

Is this counterintuitive advice? Of course. Is it even more difficult than the first piece of advice? Maybe—partly because tuning in to a certain media source may figure into a daily routine that has gone on for years.

Demand Evidence and Expertise in Your Reading and Your Writing

We suppose that most readers and most writers acquire an expectation of themselves and of others that assertions must be supported. Backing for claims varies—evidence, expert opinion, inference from consensus, presuppositions—but inquiring "How does the writer know that?" becomes routine at some points in education. But the routines and even the expectations fade unless reinforced by readers such as employers or bosses. In politics as in marketing and other pursuits, the good habits yield to expedience. For example, few users of social media bother to ask for authority or evidence for claims or arguments. Instead, cyber-banter brandishes "hot takes" and snappy comebacks, tested trolling, and the very sorts of shibboleths of which Orwell complained. Lore metastasizes. So we all must train ourselves to demand backing for claims that is as accessible, supportable, and truthful as the practical situation will permit.

Orwell indulged his antipathy to jargon, to foreign words, and to other dodges because such swindles denied readers access to the bases for claims. Acknowledging his attitude and his aptitude for phrasing his antipathy vividly, readers and writers should drill themselves to demand that writing make accessible the knowability and verifiability of key premises. Orwell excoriated euphemisms and other perversions of truth because they deprived readers and writers of assessments of the shakiness or absence of support for claims from evidence or experts. If we agree with him that almost everyone tries to ease their way around obstacles, then we ought to practice detecting in our writing signs of pretense to knowledge that we do not possess and to certainty that our readers should not honor. When we spot in our own drafts an "Arguably" at the head of a sentence, for example, we must mark that sentence for verification beyond "It might not be irrational to believe for the sake of my argument that," which is of course what "arguably" too often signals. We all ought to develop an "Orwellian" aptitude for discerning the dodging of candor.

Depending, of course, on the context, we all should respect not just Orwell's preference for the concrete over the abstract but also Orwell's preference for the demonstrable over the credible. (The abstract may be a legitimate ground for philosophical or theoretical genres.) Conscientious writers get in the habit of expecting prose to be as true as writers can make it rather than as truthy as writers dare and editors allow. In their writing they do not indulge in President Trump's "truthful hyperbole;"[19] instead, they proceed by not wanting to exaggerate in a truthy way. Conscientious writers and scrupulous readers rehearse "I don't know" or "We don't have it yet" or other mantras to remind themselves how little certainty they possess and how many puzzles remain. Honorable producers and honest consumers tell the truth as best they can and admit their doubts candidly. They base their communications in and on the concrete and the empirical. They crave accessible, confirmable documentation and admit when they cannot make available and verifiable the bases for their claims and presumptions.

In Closing

In this chapter and book, we have asked questions of Orwell's questions and behaved in an unruly way toward his rules. Let us conclude, then, by praising the spirit of his questions, which is the spirit of the conscious, self-critical, and savvy writer and of a person determined to resist such hard-wired conditioning. Much of our critique enlarged upon this spirit by adding flexibility and broader rhetorical awareness, including attention to genre, to the mix of habits to be instilled and drilled. By practicing flexibility and rhetorical awareness, we also asked tough questions about some of Orwell's rules. Indeed, we changed our minds toward such rules, which we once thought to be pretty nifty. Let us conclude by inviting you to continue to write, act, read, listen, and observe public language alertly, so that no rule, habit, or practice which exists largely for its own sake will constrict your writing, and so that you rarely if ever become an easy mark for pseudocratic language. We encourage you to remain a writer and a media-consumer who is most difficult to fool, even by your alleged allies.

Notes

1. "Politics and the English Language" bristles with passages that, we two think, suggest Orwell's posthumous assent to our enterprise. Please reread paragraphs 2, 11, and 19 in our telescoping guide.
2. We intend the pun.
3. Gordon Bowker, *Inside George Orwell: A Biography* (New York: Palgrave Macmillan, 2003), 20.
4. Bowker, *Inside George Orwell*, 176.
5. In contrast to our using genre above, our choosing a phrase both foreign and jargonistic at this juncture does violate Orwell's fifth rule. Our bad! [Our naughtiness!].
6. Please see Aristotle, *On Rhetoric: A Theory of Civic Discourse*, translated and edited by George Kennedy (New York: Oxford University Press, 1991).
7. Edward P.J. Corbett, *Classical Rhetoric for the Modern Student*, 3rd ed. (New York: Oxford University Press, 1991), 23.

8. Please recall that Orwell asserted that his five specimens were each avoidably ugly.

9. "A scrupulous writer, in every sentence that he writes, will ask himself at least four questions" might be read as other than advice to interrupt writing with questioning, but we two think that the most straightforward reading is that scrupulous writers ask questions **amid** the writing of every sentence. We two in the foregoing sentence deploy passive voice deliberately to show how the passive voice ["might be read"] discards identifying who might read the advice in some other manner and concentrates instead on how one might preserve Orwell from what he composed in haste.

10. Benjamin Bloom introduced the concept of higher-order concerns and lower-order concerns in education and it has influenced the pedagogy of composition. Benjamin Bloom, *Taxonomy of Educational Objectives, Handbook 1: Cognitive Domain* (Boston: Addison-Wesley Longman, 1956); and Lorin W. Anderson, David R. Krathwohl, Peter W. Airasian, Kathleen A. Cruikshank, Richard E. Mayer, Paul R. Pintrich, James Raths, and Merlin C. Wittrock, *A Taxonomy for Learning, Teaching, and Assessing: A Revision of Bloom's Taxonomy of Education Abridged Edition* (New York: Pearson, 2000) updated Bloom's work. A writer's constructing an argument exemplifies a higher-order concern while a writer's proofreading a late draft exemplifies a lower-order one. Both types of concerns are important, but each has a time and place.

11. We find it true but insufficient to claim that Question Six improves on Rule Six [barbarous].

12. Orwell carped against five specimen-writers for proofreading failures, so perhaps we are justified in giving Eric Arthur Blair a taste of his own medicine. However, that is not our primary aim. Rather, we maintain that useful attitudes, aptitudes, and habits are obscured by his "gumming together" queries **19 sentences** into paragraph 11.

13. We could not resist having fun with Orwell's rules and gibes. We use "ukase" to denote a proclamation by an arbitrary authority. "Ukase" is not only shorter than alternatives but covers our meaning more exactly than some longer words would. We are technically in compliance with Rule ii, then, because "ukase" will do; indeed, it does better than merely making do! What is more, it is not ancient Latin or ancient Greek! Modern writers of English derive this denigration from Russian by way of French.

14. In our view "in lieu of" works better than "in place of" because it is more idiomatically precise.

15. Orwell in the very first sentence of his second paragraph proclaims that poor writing is not just a matter of one person's skewing the facts.

16. If you have the philosophical bent to handle it, try Nicholas Turnbull, "Political Rhetoric and Its Relationship to Context: A New Theory of the Rhetorical Situation, the Rhetorical and the Political," *Critical Discourse Studies* 15, no. 12 (2016).

17. Thorstein Veblen developed the concept of "trained incapacity," which Kenneth Burke then used to argue that many capabilities, perhaps even virtues, result from drilling or willing oneself not to perceive or consider alternative perspectives. See, accessed January 22, 2017, kbjournal.org/wais.

18. This is a signal insight of Ellul in *Propaganda*.

19. Donald Trump defended "truthful hyperbole" as blameless exaggeration and effective promotion in "his" [and Tony Schwartz's] *The Art of the Deal*. We

think Orwell would have dismissed such hucksterism as beneath any writer worthy of our reading. We concede that overclaiming will often impress the gullible but urge writers to aim for a more discerning audience and readers to object to being treated like marks in a con game.

Bibliography

Anderson, Lorin W., David R. Krathwohl, Peter W. Airasian, Kathleen A. Cruikshank, Richard E. Mayer, Paul R. Pintrich, James Raths, and Merlin C. Wittrock. *A Taxonomy for Learning, Teaching, and Assessing: A Revision of Bloom's Taxonomy of Education Abridged Edition*. New York: Pearson, 2000.

Aristotle. *On Rhetoric: A Theory of Civic Discourse*. Translated and edited by George Kennedy. New York: Oxford University Press, 1991.

Bloom, Benjamin. *Taxonomy of Educational Objectives, Handbook 1: Cognitive Domain*. Boston: Addison-Wesley Longman, 1956.

Bowker, Gordon. *Inside George Orwell: A Biography*. New York: Palgrave Macmillan, 2003.

Corbett, Edward P.J. *Classical Rhetoric for the Modern Student*. 3rd ed. New York: Oxford University Press, 1991.

Trump, Donald J., and Tony Schwartz. *Trump: The Art of the Deal*. New York: Ballantine Books, 2015.

Turnbull, Nicholas. "Political Rhetoric and Its Relationship to Context: A New Theory of the Rhetorical Situation, the Rhetorical and the Political." *Critical Discourse Studies* 15, no. 12 (2016).

Index

order/lower order concerns 93; and
honesty 18, 51, 56, 101–2, 105;
"Master Habit" for 101; prefabricated
phrases in 7, 25, 27, 36, 39, 46, 48, 57;
pretentious diction in 23, 32n2, 32n5,
40, 43, 75–76, 78, 80–81, 91; *see also*
allusions, attitudes and aptitudes,
clichés, composition, directness,
discernment, essays, genres, honor,
idioms, insincerity, metaphors

xenophobia 51

For Product Safety Concerns and Information please contact our EU
representative GPSR@taylorandfrancis.com Taylor & Francis Verlag GmbH,
Kaufingerstraße 24, 80331 München, Germany

Printed and bound by CPI Group (UK) Ltd, Croydon, CR0 4YY

11/04/2025

01844009-0014